SELL
LIKE A MULE

THE GEES AND HAWS TO BECOME
A SUCCESSFUL REAL ESTATE AGENT

LISA PARDON

Dedicated to Mom and Dad,
my husband, Kent,
my children, Ashton and Logan,
and my Aunt Judy,
who have always told me,
I'm stubborn as a mule

Table of Contents

Introduction

Some lessons in life and real estate cannot be taught in the typical classroom setting. There is a great need for mentoring and training beyond simple applications. Conventional wisdom or "street smarts" is obtained through experience ... the great teacher. *Sell Like a Mule* is a practical guide for real estate agents using the metaphorical comparison of this magnificent hybrid animal, the mule. Being labeled "stubborn as a mule" is a compliment because mules are highly intelligent. What makes them stubborn? They can THINK!

The *exact* origin of the mule may be somewhat difficult to determine, but its ancestry begins with the origin of its parents, a male donkey and a female horse. This combination affords some remarkable and very desirable traits. From the father, donkeys have longevity. Some live over 50 years. They are stronger than a horse of the same size, extremely smart, and have an incredible memory. A donkey can recognize geographical areas and fellow donkeys they've not seen in 25 years. From the mother's side, horses are courageous, vigorous and agile. Using a larger mare can increase the size and stature of the mule, allowing them to carry and pull more weight. Horses are faster than donkeys, and some mules have been bred to race. When you combine the best of the donkey with the best of the horse it's easy to see why these hybrids have become highly prized.

The mule has been intentionally bred by man since ancient times and was considered the steed of choice for kings during Solomon's reign. George Washington was one of the first American mule breeders. During World Wars I and II, mules were "drafted" into active duty. They were better equipped to navigate the dense jungles and steep mountain trails that were impassible to motorized vehicles. They carried food, supplies, and ammunition into the battle zones, and they often carried wounded soldiers out of harm's way. More than 8,000 mules died in those wars, and the supply ships carrying these heroic mules were often prime targets for enemy submarines.

I first personally witnessed the brilliance of mules in the 1960s as a small child on our family farm. We had two mules, Kate and Della, who were the apple of my father's eye and his hard-working partners for growing crops. I remember many barefoot walks behind the plow, picking up arrowheads and other treasures in the freshly turned earth as Kate and Della prepared the fields for planting. The rows were always straight and perfect. They heeded Dad's verbal commands, eagerly obeying every gee and haw, turning right or left, respectively. They stood perfectly still as he adjusted their harnesses. They seemed to enjoy the work and were gentle and even-tempered giants. They never foundered or fell ill, and always required less maintenance than our horses, cows, and other farm animals.

Later, as an adult around 1994, my husband and I purchased a beautiful parcel of land in Maury County that just so happened to have once been a mule farm. We learned that many local farms in the area operated in the late 1800s breeding and supplying mules for the war effort, and for some, it was their main source of income. The area was a central hub for mule sales and gained a reputation for breeding exquisite stock. People came from all over the world to buy the prized mules, and Columbia earned the title, "Mule Capital of the World." To this day, during the first week in April, the Mule Day Festival attracts tens of thousands of tourists and international mule traders to participate in the weeklong celebration. Columbia is lovingly called "Muletown" so it's no surprise that I had to name my real estate firm Muletown Realty.

As humans, we would do well to strive for the attributes of a mule. Mules learn very quickly, often with as little as three repetitions. Their physical strength and stamina allow them to endure extreme conditions like those experienced in the front lines during the World Wars. They are the animal of choice for those steep and treacherous Grand Canyon trails and are steady and surefooted. Mules don't spook easily, and if they do, it's for good reason. They have a keen sense of self-preservation and cannot be forced to do dangerous things or work beyond their health limitations, thus, unjustly earning the reputation of being stubborn. When in fact, they are very clever and possess common sense.

Sell Like a Mule was written with the intent to help agents work smarter, not harder, to become "sure-footed" in our industry. There is much to learn, and *you don't know what you don't know.* You will need to learn how to write offers, list homes, explain contracts, navigate through home inspections, interpret appraisals, prepare for closings, manage your leads and database, and of course, how to get paid—much more than simply learning which words to fill in the contract blanks.

Psychology is involved. You must outsmart the competition. You must THINK. Conventional wisdom and knowledge must be gained quickly and with little experience. Communication skills are imperative. You will need to be intuitive, able to predict and overcome obstacles, able to understand the gee's and haw's of the industry. Additionally, you must learn to monitor and adjust your mindset—how to recognize and adapt to others' behavioral traits and personalities, how to apply time management and bring organization to your work, and lastly, how to maintain relationships so that you will have rewarding friendships, endless referrals, and repeat business for life. Indeed, you'll need many of the mule's attributes ... agility, surefootedness, strength and stamina, intelligence, memory, common sense and the ability to learn quickly, just to name a few.

Sell Like a Mule offers its readers a faster and smarter path to success, the opportunity to glean years of wisdom by learning from others' experiences and mistakes. It will create a deeper understanding of the why's and how's of real estate through the sharing of true stories from the field, both heartwarming and heart stopping. Congratulations on your decision to become a mule in a world full of horses and ponies! A career in real estate offers amazing opportunities for growth and self-development. You have opened the door to achieving substantial financial and emotional rewards, both for you and your clients. Now, it's time to become a magnificent hybrid so you can ... *Sell Like a Mule*!

"Mules have a different mindset. Although they are not as stubborn as the stereotype, they think more like a donkey than a horse. Horses react. Mules take initiative..."

~Jennifer Povey, (*Mules and Other Hybrids: About Equine Crosses, https://pethelpful.com/horses/Mules-And-Other-Hybrids-About-Equine-Crosses*)

CHAPTER 1

Mindset

Horses React, Mules Take Initiative

Let's begin with the power of mindset. Your mindset begins forming early on with your childhood experiences. You learn to move away from pain and toward pleasure. As you experience life, your mindset shapes and develops and becomes an integral part of your personality. It has a dramatic impact on your job performance, your personal relationships, and everyone with whom you come into contact. It affects how you think, your attitude, and your response to any given situation. Mindset affects your motivation, your passion, and what drives you, your "big why." It can overpower any physical attributes you have and take control, either crippling your progress or making you unstoppable.

The real estate business is often compared to riding a roller coaster. There are lots of ups and downs. You will experience extreme highs, the thrills of success and being on top of the world. Then, you will experience extreme lows, that wrenching gut feeling of failure that breaks your heart...sometimes all within a 24 hour period! How do agents ride such an emotional roller coaster and consistently come out on top? By controlling their mindset. You must learn to closely monitor your thoughts and *choose* your responses. You will find that there are two kinds of real estate agents: those that react, the horses and ponies; and those that carefully respond, the mules...thinking things through and using the power of choice to take initiative.

One of the best illustrations of this mindset control is from Stephen Covey's book, *The Seven Habits of Highly Successful People*. Mr. Covey tells the story of Victor Frankl, a psychiatrist and Jew imprisoned in a Nazi Germany death camp. He was exposed to the best and the worst of humanity. His wife, his parents, and his brother died in the camps. Only his sister survived. While there, Victor endured torture, beatings, and horrible, painful experiments on his body. He saw prisoners killing other prisoners for their food, becoming like animals ... while others gave their last ration to another, themselves going hungry. He pondered why some people reacted like animals and others, under the same conditions, chose to be compassionate. He realized he had stumbled upon the answer. It's a conscious choice. Do I react or do I respond?

He noted there is a split second in time between the stimuli (the torture in his case) and the choice of how to respond. He began his very own personal experiment to prove his theory. He learned to survive his torture by placing himself in an almost trancelike state, removing his thoughts from his body, and asking "What does this situation ask of me and what can I learn from this?" instead of, "Why me? Why is this happening to me?" He imagined himself in the future, long after the ordeal, a survivor, lecturing to his students at the university about the very torture he was experiencing and relaying to them all he had learned. Although he lost his liberty by being imprisoned and under the control of the Nazi guards, he never lost his freedom—it's a freedom we all have...the last human freedom, the power to choose how we will respond in any situation. No matter what was done to him or how horrible things became, he had the choice, the power of how he would respond. And, so do we.

A mule, when frightened, will spin in place to face the threat. They will examine the circumstances that caused their fear with careful thought and forbearance, choosing their best course of response, only running away or retreating when that is the only choice. We should do the same.

Real estate is a tough business. It will throw you a curve. You'll have to decide whether to react or whether to exercise your last human freedom, the power to choose how you will respond. I've seen many agents quit when the going got rough instead of using it as an opportunity to grow and learn. When something goes wrong, you have the capacity to learn through thoughtful initiative and to put proactive measures in place to prevent it from reoccurring. It's called failing forward...it's not a failure if you learn from it.

Your thoughts matter. In truth, thoughts *are* matter. Thoughts have energy, a form of energy created in our brains that have so much power over our bodies that thoughts, alone, can determine our successes and failures. Thoughts precede our actions, both consciously and subconsciously. When you have a thought, whether positive or negative, an electro-chemical reaction starts. Energy is created, and a chemical substance called endorphin is released in your brain. Endorphins are morphine-like chemicals, naturally produced by your body that help limit pain while triggering positive feelings. It's the brain's reward system.

Imagine you are walking through a field of tall grass. As you pass through the field for the first time, you leave a path as the grass folds down beneath your steps. As you pass through that same path again, more grass lies down, and the path becomes wider, deeper and easier to navigate. You can move more quickly. Each time you move down the path it enlarges and becomes more like a well-traveled road. Now, envision a "thought" making a path through your brain. Each time that specific thought occurs, it passes through the same path, and with each repetition, the path becomes wider and deeper and easier to navigate. The path of the thought becomes like a road and then, a super highway. This explains why you might have some thoughts repetitively, quickly traveling through your brain, until they become habitual, even addictive. When the thought is a limiting belief or a negative and destructive dialogue from your inner voice, it becomes necessary to create a new thought, to forge a new path so that the old path will become overgrown and less traveled.

Let's examine the neuroscience behind the thought process. When you have a thought, an electrical signal moves along your brain's axons like a wave. Axons form the connections between neurons. When the wave reaches the end of the axon, chemical neurotransmitters are released into the synapse, a chemical junction shared by the axon tip and target neuron. The target neuron then sends out an electrical impulse that spreads to other neurons, and within a matter of seconds, the signal has spread to billions of neurons throughout your brain causing a cascade of chemical release that affects your mood.

Whether the thought is negative or positive, you can still become addicted to the process. Your brain craves the chemical release, even if the thought is horrible and harmful. Although it's impossible to prevent a thought from popping into your head, you can replace it with a more pleasant thought. Don't let superhighways of negative thoughts be forged into your brain and limit your chances for success. A mule shows initiative and responds instead of reacting. You must spin in place and assess your thoughts and fears.

Our thoughts have energy. Have you ever heard someone say bad things come in threes? It's because of the law of attraction. If you focus your thoughts on the negative, you attract that same kind of energy. If you focus on the positive, you attract positive energy. Dianna Kokozska, CEO and founder of Maps

Coaching for Keller Williams Realty says, "What you focus on expands." It's one of her *BOLD* laws. So, whether you focus on the bad or the good, that's what you will get more of. Here's an exercise to prove it. Imagine you are driving down a road. Now fix your eyes on a large tree just to the right up ahead. Focus and keep staring at the tree. You will find that your car will begin to veer off and steer toward the tree, without your consciously moving the steering wheel. The power of attraction is pulling you directly toward your focus, the tree.

Perhaps you know a "Debbie Downer." This person can bring gloom and doom into the room just by entering. Nothing good ever seems to happen to them. They are always in a crisis. Their deal fell through, they are sick, or their car is broken. Bad things follow them around like a dark cloud overhead. On the opposite end of the spectrum, you may know someone who lights up the room when he or she enters. This person radiates confidence and positive energy and seems to attract everything good in life. They are resilient, even in trying times, and are always grateful.

Why is their mindset so different? Is it because bad things have happened to one and not the other? Certainly not. Everyone has hard times. We never know what others are going through. Using the lessons of Victor Frankl, "Debbie Downer" is living in victim mode, asking "Why me?" instead of "What is expected of me in this situation?" Her negative energy will attract more of the same, a very good reason for choosing to think positively when times are tough. When we ask what it is that is required of us and what we can learn from this, we grow from the experience, even at times, grateful that the misfortune has occurred. Gratitude is one of the highest positive energies and will attract more positive energy; focus on good things and they will begin to happen more often than bad things.

Dr. Masaru Emoto (1943–2014) was a Japanese author, photographer, and researcher who claimed that the energy from thoughts had an actual physical effect on the molecular structure of water. His research sought to prove that water reacts differently to positive and negative thoughts. In his most famous experiment, he used distilled water purified for hospital use, all produced by the same company so there would be no variable. Each vial of water was labeled and exposed to a thought, be it positive or negative. Then the water was frozen so that ice crystals could form. The results were astounding. His crew of researchers observed beautiful and intricate ice crystal formation in the water where good thoughts were labeled on the vials…thoughts like "God," "peace," "joy," and "love." They noted similar crystal formation in the vials over which they played soothing music and also over those which they offered prayer.

On the other hand, they observed disfigured and hideous crystal formations, some even resembling a monstrous face, in those vials exposed to negative thoughts like "hate," "anger," "death," "evil," and "Satan." Moreover, they never once observed any two identical crystal formations in any of the test vials. The results are published as photograph collections: *Messages from Water 1* (1999), *Messages from Water 2* (2002), *Messages from Water 3* (2004), and *Messages from Water 4* (2008). (Hado Kyoiku-Sha publishing.) Then in November 2001, *Water Knows the Answer* (Sunmark Publishing) gave even more explanation about the actual research results. His research pointed to an amazing discovery, actually seeing the physical effect of thoughts on water. Just because we cannot see our thoughts doesn't mean they don't have powerful energy.

Since our bodies are made up of 60% water. Do you see the connection? What type of crystals would you formulate? Many doctors and nurses have seen illnesses unexplainably cured through prayer and positive thought. They will quickly tell you a great attitude is the most important factor in recovery from serious illness and injury. Your thoughts do, indeed, have energy. And only you can choose the kind of energy you allow. What will your mindset be when the going gets rough?

As you experience life, you will develop behavior patterns and responses that can be positive and encouraging or they can be self-limiting and destructive. The choice is yours, but only if you learn to take control of your inner conversation, your thoughts. One of my favorite quotes is by Bryant H. McGill. He says it best, "The worst bully you will ever encounter in life are your own thoughts."

One more story about mindset...

The story of John James Audubon (1785–1851) is a great example of controlling your inner conversation and learning from failure. Audubon was a famous artist and ornithologist noted for his studies of American birds. Whenever he would go on a business trip, he would leave at home his box containing over 200 of his meticulously drawn bird illustrations, each one finely detailed and back-dropped in their natural habitats. Once, after a trip, he returned home to find that rats had chewed through the box and eaten holes in all his papers. Years and years of his work had been destroyed. He was devastated for weeks, unable to accept what had happened, nearly paralyzed in his despair. Until one morning, he decided his attitude must change. He gathered his art supplies and headed back to the woods. He made a conscious choice to accept what had happened and to use this to grow. He decided to look at the destruction of the years of work as an opportunity to start over, to make the drawings better than before.

After suffering this major setback, John James Audubon soon completed his most famous work, *The Birds of America*. Your attitude can make or break you, just as it did for John James Audubon. You may not be a famous artist, but you will spend hours and even days and weeks putting a deal together just to have it fall through. You will probably experience the same initial response as Audubon. Just don't stay there. Get up, start again, and learn from the experience. Be grateful for the opportunity to grow.

If you want more positive energy in your life, gratitude is one of the most powerful emotions you can have. It's very hard to feel negative when you are grateful. Here are two proven strategies to stay in gratitude. First, use affirmations. Affirmations are your spoken convictions that send positive reinforcement to your subconscious. They are the positive thoughts that create a new path so that the old path of self-doubt and discouragement fades away. If you are feeling overwhelmed or tired, a good affirmation to say is, "I have all the energy I need to have a great and productive day, and I will get my most important tasks completed." If you are fearful and lack confidence as you head to your listing appointment, you could say, "I've got this listing if I want it, and I'm totally prepared so that the sellers can easily see they should hire me." No matter what obstacle you are facing, look for a positive affirmation. Top agents use daily affirmations because in this industry you will face some tough obstacles, and it takes proper mental preparation to stay on top of your game.

A second proven strategy to stay in gratitude is to know your "Big Why." Everyone has a "Big Why." It's that self-motivation that comes from knowing what moves you. Your "why" could be driven by any number of things...like love, survival, anger, vengeance, financial gain, security, or fear. If you've ever seen the movie, "Gone with The Wind," you will remember the scene where Scarlet O'Hara is so hungry she runs into the barren field, uproots a lone radish and falls to the ground, eating it raw, dirt and all. She gags and spits out the turnip, pulls herself together and raises her fist to the sky and swears, "With God as my witness, I'll never go hungry again." At that moment her "Big Why" was to never endure that type of pain, to never be hungry again … and she was prepared to do whatever it took … whether that meant crafting a dress from draperies or marrying a man she didn't love for his money.

Vengeance may not be the best "Big Why," but it gets the job done in this next example. A long-suffering wife who finally gathered the courage to divorce her abusive husband stood facing him as he smirked and said to her, "You'll never amount to anything. You'll never be able to make it without me. You don't have a job. You never even graduated high school. No one will ever want you because you are fat and ugly." She stared back at him in horror and disbelief that she could ever have loved someone so cruel and hateful. She decided at that moment her new reason for living was to show him just how wrong he was. Her "Big Why" became her all-encompassing passion. She found a strength she didn't know she had, and she worked two jobs, went back to school, got her GED, and became a very successful real estate broker, and of course, wealth followed. She found the love of her life, and they married and lived very happily. All because of her desire to show him he was wrong. Obviously, after accomplishing her goal her "Big Why" changed. In the same way, your Big Why will evolve over time as your life experiences change.

Love can be a driving force for many "Big Why's". A couple I attend church with felt led to sell their home in the U.S and use the money to further their mission work in India. I watched as they sold their beautiful home and used the proceeds to help an orphanage and many needy souls in a far away country.

So, what drives *you*? Everyone has a purpose, a "Big Why." It's time for some inner reflection to find your reason for doing what you do. Why are you in real estate? Is it a child you want to send to college? Are there elderly parents you want to care for? Is there a new car or dream vacation in your future? Do you want to prove you've got what it takes? Has no one in your family ever found financial success, and you want to be the first? Do you want a career where you can spend every day helping others accomplish their goals and improve their quality of life? When you identify your "Big Why," you will find the courage and determination to do whatever it takes to accomplish it.

Albert Einstein said, "Imagination is everything. It is the preview of life's coming attractions." Everything you see that is man-made is something that started off in someone's imagination. Why not design the life you want in your imagination and start visualizing your coming attractions right now? Once you've determined your "Big Why" here is an exercise to keep it top of mind. On a poster board, or on your computer screen if you prefer to make it digitally, make a vision board with pictures of what drives you. What is your motivation? What are your dreams?

My vision board has a picture of my husband and me, our two grown children, my widowed aunt and mom, a Bible, a beautiful beach scene, some Spanish words, a weight goal, and a log cabin. Each of these visuals represents a goal or dream I intend to accomplish. It's my "Why." I am in real estate because I love my family. I want to spend quality time with my husband and children, to be able to care for my mom and aunt financially and emotionally. I want to learn a new language, to teach art lessons and to dabble in antiques. I want to construct a log cabin on our farm, beside my home, and I want to study the Bible and understand more deeply and to bring others closer to God. Get the picture?

Place your vision board where you will see it every day and update it as your "Why" evolves. Hang it on the refrigerator, the wall in your office or tape it to your bathroom mirror. Save it as your screensaver on your phone or computer. Put it in a place where it is likely to be seen every single day so that it reminds you why it's important to get up, get dressed, and show up, even on those days you don't feel like it. Every day you must imagine in your mind how wonderful it will feel when you reach your "Why."

Don't forget, just like you, your real estate clients have a "Big Why." There is a reason why they are selling or buying that house. Find out what it is. Are they scaling back, or needing a larger home? Are they relocating to be closer to family? You need to ask the right questions and dig deep when interviewing buyers and sellers until they share their motivation behind their decision to buy or sell. They'll most likely be glad to share their dreams and goals and their reason for making the move. You must understand what motivates them and what they are trying to accomplish so that you can work toward their goal as a team. Teamwork is the ability to work together toward a common vision...and no one does it better than mules!

"Mules are very smart. They are thinkers. They instinctively size up a situation and take the most direct path. They are wary as they use their ears to listen and scope out what is going on around them. They are rarely deterred once a decision is made. They either plant their feet, refusing to move, or go in the direction they choose … Some people use the phrase **stubborn as a mule** *to describe someone in a negative light. I have been called that many times. I like to think of myself as deliberate, consistent, a thinker, strong, and with endurance."*

~Karen Hoyt *(Stubborn as a Mule, https://beta.hepmag.com/blog/hepatitisc-stubborn-mule)*

CHAPTER 2

Building Rapport and Connecting with Your Clients

Mules Have Very Large Ears to Listen With

You've probably heard the saying, "People feel more comfortable doing business with people they know and trust." We tend to respect the experience and advice given from someone we feel rapport with, and we are more likely to value their contribution to the decision-making process. In rare occasions rapport happens naturally. Have you ever met a person and for some reason you liked them instantly? Most of the time rapport will have to be built over time.

There are three fundamental techniques to building rapport: 1) Mirror and Matching; 2) Using the D.I.S.C. Profile; and 3) Active Listening.

Mirror and Matching – A mule observes and follows the lead.

Mirror and matching techniques work at the subconscious level. It is based on the premise that people like people who have similarities to them. Observe the person you're talking to. Watch their body language, vocal speed, volume, and even their word choice. If they cross their arms or legs, very subtly cross yours in the same manner. If they lean forward, you lean slightly forward. If they use a lot of hand gestures, you should do likewise. Change the volume and speed of your voice to match theirs, as well. If they're talking slowly and in a lowered voice, you do the same. Likewise, if they are talking fast and in an animated way, match them. Be careful that you don't overdo your mirror and matching and never mimic an accent because that could cause offense.

Obviously, mirroring and matching doesn't guarantee that a customer will hire you and do business with you. The goal is for them to be more comfortable with you and, therefore, more open to your influence in the decision-making process. This technique must be practiced and perfected so it seems natural. Don't "wing it" on a customer. Practice with a friend or family member until you feel at ease with the process and it seems natural.

Using the D.I.S.C. Profile to Build Rapport – Mules have individual distinct personalities.

Because you are in sales, one of the most valuable skills you need to learn is how to recognize and adapt to the different personality styles of people. The ability to connect with your client is key. Knowing their preferred style of communication leads to better conversations and allows you to quickly build rapport and trust. The D.I.S.C. personality assessment can help you understand not only *your* dominant personality trait, but it can also help you quickly identify those of your clients. The D.I.S.C. profile test developed by William Marston is divided into four distinct personality types: (D) Dominance, (I) Influence, (S) Steadiness, and (C) Correctness or Compliance.

All D.I.S.C. styles have areas of strengths and weaknesses. There are no right or wrong styles, and it does not limit what you can accomplish or how successful you can be. Your D.I.S.C. style is only a prediction of how you tend to do things. We are all a mixture of these traits and can even change over the years through the impact of circumstances and experiences. You can find very successful people represented in all four D.I.S.C. types. It is important to recognize these styles so that you will not only know who *you* are, but who others are so that you can adapt your style to best interact with them. Mules have resilience and adaptability because they have a wonderful mixture of all the personality styles. They can lead or follow, analyze and respond to data, or just spontaneously kick up their heels. They are most always careful and health conscious, and

25

many times playful and endearing. Examine the four behavioral styles and see if you can determine which one is your dominant personality trait.

(D) Dominance. D's are your movers and shakers. They are driven, decisive, wanting to get quickly to the bottom line, dominant, daring, and not afraid to take risks. They are aggressive and demanding. They are confident, maybe even overconfident at times. Most CEOs, leaders, and presidents of organizations are D's. They would rather lead than follow, and they do an excellent job of leading. It's a good that only about 10% of the population are D's, or we'd be constantly butting heads over who is going to be the leader. They are not chatty on the phone and can be viewed as blunt. They will quickly say, "Get to the point, please" or "Give me the short version." They are not very good listeners, often interrupting. D's are result oriented, bottom-line thinkers, and quick concluders. They are willing to take risks and want to get things done now, so they will make snap decisions. They embrace change and love competition and challenges. D's can be perceived to be impatient and overbearing because they want things done quickly and done their way. They excel at seeing the big picture and multi-tasking. Their biggest fear is that their time will be wasted. As a result, even the most kindhearted D may come across as rude, blunt, aggressive and demanding. You must understand that spending too much time on one thing is not in their DNA. Some famous D's are David Letterman, Donald Trump, Hillary Clinton, Tiger Woods, Rosie O'Donnell,

Coach Bobby Knight, Madonna, and Captain Kirk of *Star Trek*. (Speaker Net News, David Greenberg) The animal examples of a D are the Horse and the Lion.

(I) Influence. I's are your cheerleaders and encouragers, eternal optimists, the glass is always half full kind of people. Those who exhibit the traits of an I tend to be people-oriented, and they make up approximately 32% of the population. They inspire people and have influence and persuasion. They can align others to get things done so they are great recruiters for volunteer groups and events. Impulsive and lovers of spontaneity, they may overpromise in order to be liked and then not be able to perform. For example, the mom at the PTA who holds up her hand when the speaker asks who can make 200 cupcakes for a school fundraiser by 5:00 p.m. the next day, even though her plate is so full she can't fit one more thing on it. Some people perceive I's as flighty and disorganized because they are doing so many different things at the same time. They are the social butterflies who never meet a stranger and can strike up a conversation with anyone. I's love socializing and can talk for hours, if you let them, and they are always up for something new and different, because to them, change is exciting. I's are open hearted and value relationships. They tend to focus more on people and less on details. Their biggest fear is rejection, that someone won't like them because they want and need everyone to like them. Some famous I's you may recognize are Robin Williams, Bill Clinton, Ellen DeGeneres, Prince Harry, Will Smith, Dr. McCoy of *Star Trek*, Steve Martin, Oprah Winfrey, and Jay Leno. (Speaker Net News, David Greenberg) A great animal example of an "I" is the Dog, our most social animal, wanting only to please.

(S) Steadiness. S's are your tried and true, calm, easy-going people with a keen sense of fair play. S's are very people oriented and make up about 30% of the world's population. They are always the same every time you meet them, no drama, and steady as you go. No extreme highs and lows, just dependable and steadfast. S's are great cooperators and make excellent team members. However, they prefer you to tell them what, when, and how you want the task completed, and they love checklists. If you don't give them enough detail they may be fearful of making a mistake and late to start. They are sincere in what they say and can be trusted to follow through with actions they promise. S's love security. They are more thoughtful of others and tend to keep their word and agreements. S's are less spontaneous and spend much time and thought in decision-making. They consider others and focus on agreements. They prefer people they already know and tend to be reserved. Family and friends are very important to S's. Their biggest fear is the loss of stability, and therefore, they will resist change. Why fix it if it's not broken, and why rock the boat if everything is just fine, status quo? Some famous S's are Peyton Manning, Jimmy Fallon, Mr. Sulu of *Star Trek*, Michael J. Fox, Mahatma Ghandi, Barbara Bush, Halle Berry, and Jimmy Carter. (Speaker Net News, David Greenberg) Ants are our animal S's through and through and exhibit great teamwork.

(C) Correctness and Compliance. C's demonstrate the most analytical and reserved style. C's tend to be task related, very detail-oriented, and make up 28% of the world's population. They want the facts, information, and proof needed to draw the right conclusion. They don't mind working alone. Some professions where C's excel are accountants, engineers, architects, doctors, astronauts, and pilots. They have very high standards, pay great attention to detail, and tend to focus on mistakes. They can come across as critical to others. They can easily over analyze a situation and would rather take an excessive amount of time in doing it right the first time than to do it over. Quality and accuracy are most important to them. They rely on expertise and competency and want everything to be precise and correct. Their decision-making is black and white with no shades of grey. It's either wrong or right. They want to control as much as they can in their environment so that they know the outcome will be accurate and the desired quality. Their closet may be color coordinated and organized. C's clothing will be subdued, mostly black and white or navy, and they rarely wear flamboyant colors. All the cans are facing the front and stacked neatly in their pantry shelves. They have routines and like to stick to them. A C's garage and car may be highly organized. They plan their itinerary completely, even vacations, and have difficulty being spontaneous. A C's biggest fear is to make a mistake. They will adapt to change with proof, but only after much analyzing and thought. C's are the most reserved of all the styles. Some famous C's are Bill Gates, Sherlock Holmes, Richard Nixon, Clint Eastwood,

Albert Einstein, Hermione of *Harry Potter*, Condoleezza Rice, and Spock of *Star Trek*. (Speaker Net News, David Greenberg) Most Cats require evidence and will need to be coaxed and convinced and are definitely C's in our animal kingdom.

How do these personality styles translate to real estate? Which of the four styles do you think would be the hardest to get to write an offer on a new home? The answer is simple, the S's. When you are working with an S you need to anticipate their hesitation and fear to make a commitment to change. Buying or selling a home is one of the biggest changes they will face in their lifetime. You will need to be both patient and vigilant in helping them along. If you have a buyer who keeps going back to the same house, even after looking at five more homes, that's your cue they're stuck, unable to commit to the change, even though they want the house and you know it! You might guide them along by saying, "I know you love this house. Let's make a list of your concerns, and we'll get the answers. Then we can either eliminate this home or move forward and make it yours."

I had an S client that woke up in the middle of the night and called me to cancel the sale. She experienced fear and remorse and kept saying, "What have I done? I love this house. I may not be happy in my new neighborhood." As we talked through it, I discovered it was just her fear of change. I learned a powerful lesson. In the future I will prepare my S's ahead of time with a conversation that goes something like this, "Sue, I know you are excited right now that we have an accepted offer on your home. Let's talk about what may happen. Tonight, after dinner, when the kids are in bed and you are settling in for the night, you may wake up in a panic and think, '*What have I done?*' Let me assure you this is normal. You have a lot of wonderful memories in this home, and it's been a great place to raise your family. It's a natural reaction I've seen many times. Just don't second guess yourself and think you've made a mistake in selling your home. If this happens, I want you to concentrate on how wonderful it will be when your family is moved into your new home and you finally have that backyard of your dreams. It's going to be great having your children's friends over with lots of space for sleepovers and campouts. If that panicky feeling hits you, here's my number. Just call me, even if it's 2 in the morning. I'll talk you off the ledge. I'm here to help."

You've told her it's normal so when that thought does occur, she'll be ready for it. You've brought her back to her "Big Why", and there's less chance of the anxiety derailing the sale. Don't get me wrong, I never try and persuade a client to go ahead with a sale if it's not in their best interest. There may be legitimate reasons why they can't go through with the sale, and that's okay. I'm only referring to the generalized anxiety of change an S may experience.

If you are dealing with a D, you will want to be direct and to the point with your conversations. Always respond immediately and be on time for every appointment. Never hold up the process when working with a D. Give them options wherever possible and allow them to choose so they feel in control. Keep all communications, including emails, brief, precise and clear. And get ready for a quick sale because D's can decide to buy the first home they look at. Remember, they make spontaneous decisions easily.

When working with an "I", remember to allow extra time for visiting and socializing. You will need to take them to lunch, call them in the evenings, and stay very much in touch with them. Friend them on their favorite social media platform. You will need to narrow down their wants and needs as much as possible so they will stay on track. Give them lots of counsel so they don't make an impulsive purchase that won't work for them. And don't neglect them after the sale or they'll feel rejected and used, or that the relationship was only about the business. Keep it fun and interesting like having them give a nickname to each home as they view them (which is a good idea regardless of the personality type).

When working with a C, make sure you supply them with all the information you can acquire on the homes they are interested in. Include the tax records, CMAs (comparative market analysis), property disclosures, and overhead satellite views, and throw in some charts and stats including demographics of the area for them to mull over. Always ask for the costs of utilities because a C will want to know about the monthly expenses. Keep records of all the homes you show them, be ready to do research and request more information for them. C's usually have a good understanding of technology so give them sources online where they can personally research further. Patience and endurance are key when working with C's. It takes them longer to gather all the information, so don't expect an impulse buy, even if the home is perfect for them. Given enough information or "proof" they will move forward.

Another way the personality styles translate to your business is in their sense of time. I am a high I personality, so I am notoriously overestimating how much time I have left before my next appointment. I think I can always do one more project before I leave. I tend to get caught up in the conversation, so it's not unusual for me to lose my sense of time and be running late. I have learned to adjust by setting my watch ahead by 15 minutes. This gets me out the door on time. Sometimes I set an alarm on my phone. Punctuality is very important, it reflects your level of professionalism. An S will always be on time. You can count on them to show up when they say they will. A D personality expects you to be on time as they don't like their time wasted. However, to a C, "on time" is 15 minutes *early* so that you can start at the exact time of the appointment. Being late to an appointment with a C makes a terrible impression and is a good way of losing them as a client forever.

It's obvious that personalities are more complex and multidimensional than simply falling into four basic D.I.S.C. styles. The D.I.S.C. Model gives people a common base or language to better understand themselves and others. Understanding is key to good communication and relationships. Make sure you know who you are and to whom you are speaking. It really does make a difference in how you connect with others.

There are several resources for taking the D.I.S.C Assessment online if your brokerage doesn't offer it in-house. Make sure you take the assessment to self-discover how to become a better communicator and build valuable and lasting relationships with others.

Active Listening

Listening is one of the most important skills you need in building rapport. The average person only hears 25% of what is said. Think of what you are missing! The ability to which you can listen is a major factor to your success in your career, and more importantly, the quality of your relationships with others. Active listening involves your full focus and concentration. It is making a conscious effort to not only hear the words, but more importantly, to hear and understand the message being conveyed during the conversation.

The talking stick has been used for centuries by many American Indian tribes and is the greatest example of active listening. Imagine a Pow-Wow and sitting in the circle are warriors and chiefs. Only one person can speak and only while he holds the talking stick; the others must remain silent. The leading elder holds the stick and begins speaking. Only when he feels that what he has to say is understood will he hold out the talking stick. And then the next one will take it and speak until he feels his message is also understood. No one has to agree with him, just understand what is being expressed. In this manner, the stick is passed from one individual to the next until everyone who wants to speak has the opportunity. No interruptions or argued points are allowed while someone holds the stick. The talking stick assures the speaker that he has everyone's focus and the message will be understood.

When you practice active listening, you must fully focus on what is being said. You must block out any distractions and not think about your reply while others are still speaking. Acknowledge you are listening, nod your head, lean forward. Listen to their words and pay attention to their body language. When they have finished speaking, paraphrase what they said. Ask questions to ensure you have understood the message.

Mary Kay Ash is attributed as saying, "Pretend that every single person you meet has a sign around his or her neck that says 'Make me feel important.' Not only will you succeed in sales, you will succeed in life." There is no better way to make someone feel important than to value what they are saying and truly listen. Why do you think a mule has such very large ears? They are for listening.

"You'll never plow a field by turning it over in your mind."

~Irish Proverb

CHAPTER 3

Lead Generation
Blinders Help a Mule Stay on Path

One of the first obstacles you will face as a real estate agent is how to attract customers. You must learn which actions or processes will find and cultivate potential customers. Instead of spending tons of money on marketing and expensive advertising, it is recommended to prospect for leads. Prospecting is less expensive. It requires you to spend *time* instead of *money*. Prospecting requires making phone calls, writing notes, door knocking, and making in-person visits to get leads. Leads are the beginning of your revenue stream. You will need a steady flow of leads to convert into appointments and, ultimately, contracts. If the stream of leads stops flowing, your business will dry up like a barren riverbed.

Gary Keller, at the helm of Keller Williams Realty, International, and author of *The Millionaire Real Estate Agent* and *The One Thing*, uses the visual of a funnel-shaped pipeline to illustrate the process of finding leads and converting them to closings. A steady stream of leads pours into the larger top of the funnel; there's a mathematical formula...out of every 200 leads, maybe 10 will result in an appointment. This is typical for agents just getting started. Remember, not every appointment will result in a signed agreement and not every agreement will result in a closed sale.

So how many leads do you need? The answer is you will need a lot! You must constantly be feeding leads into the top of the funnel to keep the pipeline full. Make sure you are focusing your efforts on the activities that will produce the highest conversion rate. For example, if you are generating leads from your personal sphere (people who already know and like you), you may only need to contact ten to fifteen of these close acquaintances to get one lead. In contrast, lead generating to strangers may take as many as 50 to 100 contacts to generate one lead. Prospecting to your personal sphere nets you one lead out of every ten contacts. That's a 1/10 conversion rate. Prospecting to strangers nets you one lead out of every 50 contacts, if you're lucky. That's a 1/50 conversion rate. Obviously, your time and efforts will net more leads when you are prospecting from your personal sphere.

I was attending a training class for Productivity Coaches when Toni Dicello of Maps Coaching (Keller Williams Realty) made a profound statement ... that real estate agents should adopt the following mindset, "You wake up every morning and you are unemployed; that is, until you have an appointment." My recommendation is to identify a minimum of ten leads to contact every day. From those leads, schedule three appointments for the week. These are your job interviews. Not every appointment will convert to a signed agreement, but you will improve over time and should begin getting one to two signed agreements from those three appointments. The objective is to increase your skills in building rapport, asking the right questions, and knowing how to address any objections they may have.

All leads are good leads if they eventually convert to business. Some leads take longer to convert than others. In real estate, a *hot lead* is a lead who is ready, willing, and able to buy or sell a property immediately, within 30 days or less. Anything that takes longer than 30 days is a *warm lead*, and, if longer than 60 days, it's a *cold lead* or a *nurture*.

You may spend weeks, or even months showing a client homes before they find the perfect one, get it under contract, and hopefully close. The work you do today is what produces your income 30 to 60 days from now. Experienced agents have learned to juggle several clients together, at the same time, with sales at different stages in both the closing and beginning stages. And, you need all three types of leads (hot, warm and nurture) to keep the pipeline full. Lots of work and preparation is done ahead of your commission, and it must be done every day, consistently, if you want to have a steady flow of income. You don't find a buyer and close the same day; the work you do today produces your income 30 to 60 days later. It's a basic principle that does not change.

I like to use the analogy of my brother, Bobby, a farmer, to explain this basic principle. He begins preparing for the next growing season during the winter. He works on the farm equipment, and he makes repairs to the buildings and tools in preparation for the spring planting. He makes the final decisions about what crops to plant and in which fields to plant them. He turns the earth, adds fertilizer to the fields, and plants cover crops to protect the soil. In the springtime, he tills the fields again and plants the crops in perfectly straight rows. He fertilizes again and then manages the weeds. There's lots of watering, and he must keep a watch out for the weather. He's been working all year to get paid from the harvest. What if Bobby skipped all the preparation steps in the winter and spring and went straight for the harvest in the summer and fall? Obviously, he wouldn't have any crops to harvest. It's silly to think a farmer would skip all the preparation. Then why do agents tend to skip the vital preparation steps to their harvest?

In the same way that Bobby works on his equipment, buildings, and tools, you must develop your brand and get your business cards, name badges, and your web site ready for business. Just as Bobby makes final decisions about the crops, you must make decisions as to the type of business you would like. Would you like to work with first-time homebuyers? Land? New construction? Investments? Or maybe a combination of these. Now, instead of turning the earth, you must lead generate and prospect for leads. Instead of fertilizing the field, you cultivate the lead, build rapport, ask the right questions, give the right answers, and convert your appointments into a signed agreement. Instead of working to manage the weeds, water, and weather, you manage the transaction and provide the highest level of service to your client. Then comes the harvest. You get paid!

Where do you start? How do you find the time to lead generate? Schedule it! Dianna Kokoszka, CEO and founder of Maps Coaching, Keller Williams Realty, says, "If it's not in your schedule, it doesn't exist." It's another of her *BOLD* laws. This is so true! The most successful agents spend a minimum of two hours a day prospecting for leads. You must focus like a mule wearing blinders and remove every obstacle that could steer you off course. Find a quiet place to conduct your lead generation. Build a bunker so you won't be disturbed. Then, time block lead generation into your daily schedule, ideally at the same time each day, preferably mornings because that is when most of us have our highest energy. For example, in your calendar set aside Mondays through Fridays from 9:00 a.m. to 11:00 a.m. solely for lead generation; not for reading emails, running errands, or checking social media. During this time, pick up your phone, call your sphere, network, knock on doors, write letters, all the while carefully guarding that you only do lead generation activities. No responding to your emails or posting on social media during your lead generation time.

Now that you have lead generation time blocked in your calendar, here are the 10 most effective forms of lead generation successful agents use.

1. Begin with your sphere

The fastest leads start with who you already know? People like doing business with people they know; therefore, the people in your inner sphere are your biggest fans. Most of them are willing to help and will hire your services, or at the very least, recommend you to a friend or family member who needs your help. Chances are your first client will be a family member, a close friend, or a coworker, so it's a natural place to start.

Your sphere of influence is the beginning of your database, your most valuable business asset. It's important to organize your database so that you can easily access names, addresses, phone numbers, emails, and social media accounts so that you can connect with them in as many ways as possible. Group them into categories that will help you connect more efficiently. For example, some of my groups are family, local agents, out of state agents, vendors (i.e. electricians, plumbers, automotive repair, doctors, and personal service providers), neighbors, neighborhoods, and friends. The goal is to communicate with and add 10 names each day to your database so you can quickly increase your inner sphere of advocates.

Within your sphere, you will want to have a few *core* advocates. A core advocate is someone who will use you and recommend you for real estate services. However, they are in a job or position where they can feed you many more leads than your normal advocate, and their referrals will help you grow your business exponentially. One of my core advocates sent me dozens of clients over a period of three years. My husband owned a veterinary hospital, and they constantly had a flow of new clients moving into the area. His receptionist would ask them to fill out a questionnaire while creating their client file. If new to the area, she would ask them how they liked their new home, and if the topic of searching for a house came up, she would pull out one of my business cards and say, "I know just who you need to call. This is Dr. Pardon's wife, and she'll take very good care of you." She sent me fresh leads almost every week. Core advocates are golden. You will want to thank them each time for sending the leads, whether or not that lead converts to business. Although real estate regulations will not allow cash reimbursement for referrals, you can always find a way to say thank you. Homemade pies and cakes, lunch outings, coffee, handwritten notes, and random acts of kindness show them how much you appreciate their referrals.

If you are a new agent, now is the time to announce to your sphere that you've started a career in real estate. And once you've told them about your new venture, periodically remind them. Call them, drop by, visit, email, or even better, send them a letter. Here's an example of an announcement letter you can send to your sphere:

Dear _____,

Because of our (*friendship, relationship, acquaintance, etc.*), I wanted you to be one of the first to know that I now have my real estate license and am an associate broker with (*name of firm*). Although I am new to real estate, I have intentionally aligned myself with a team of experienced agents so that my clients will have the enthusiasm and passion that comes with being a new agent without having to sacrifice the wisdom and experience that comes with someone who has many years in the industry. You can rest assured that I am offering a 10+ level of service to all my clients. Whether you are a first-time homebuyer or a seasoned investor, I can help you navigate through the transaction with ease and take the stress out of buying or selling in this real estate market. You can rely on my professional counsel and market knowledge to guide you every step of the way.

Since the stock market is unpredictable and the housing market is strong, many people are thinking about buying or selling a home or investing in real estate this year. I am here to help with cutting edge technology, effective marketing, and internet distribution, and I can be a source of preferred vendors to help with repairs and renovations. Please know that I promise to bring value with my service and will be contacting you to provide relevant updates on the real estate market, as well as offering helpful information like market changes and homes selling in your area.

If you or anyone you know needs real estate services, please remember me. When you refer a client to me, you have my assurance that I will treat them like family, providing professional service they can depend on and handling their transaction with integrity and perseverance, utilizing the strong negotiation and mediation skills that I have learned over the years. (My mom tells me I've been a fierce negotiator since I was three years old.)

If you ever have any questions about real estate, don't hesitate to contact me. I welcome the opportunity to assist you.

I look forward to speaking with you soon. I've enclosed a few of my cards in case you have a friend who may need help with real estate. Much of the success of my new business depends on referrals like the ones I will be getting from my family and friends. Thank you in advance for being willing to recommend me!

(Put your signature and company information and be sure to include a few of your business cards.)

2. Network in your community

What if you are new to the area and you don't have a local sphere of influence? Networking can help build a database. We think of football and soccer as being contact sports. Lead generation is very much a contact sport. Networking offers an opportunity for face-to-face interaction with potential clients. You want to make a good impression, so before you begin networking, do a mindset check. Are you ready and confident? Do you know what you are going to say?

A good way to build confidence before a networking situation or event is to practice your "elevator pitch." An elevator pitch is a short dialogue about your unique value proposition. The objective is to be able to recite your UVP in one minute or less. Your UVP is a clear and concise statement that describes the benefit the client will receive from hiring you, how you will solve your customer's needs, and what sets you apart from the competition. Your UVP is the key to earning their business. Integrity and relationships are important, but if people don't see you as valuable, they will never do business with you. What sets the agent apart in the announcement letter? What's their value? Their UVP conveys, "I am passionate about service, knowledgeable about the area, and easily accessible. I collectively have experience, am a strong negotiator, and can navigate through any transaction, reducing stress and minimizing problems. I have excellent and consistent communication procedures in place. I can get the job done."

Take the time to develop and write your own unique value proposition. Have it ready for any occasion. Metaphorically, you never know when that elevator door will open and there stands before you the client opportunity of a lifetime. Be ready, know your UVP.

Now that you are ready to make a good impression, it's time to network! There are many ways for face-to-face interaction.

You can attend small business conferences. These are great ways to meet other local business owners and create opportunities for valuable connections. Join community and volunteer groups. Join the local Chamber of Commerce, Rotary, Civitan, Kiwanis, and other clubs. Volunteer at the Boys and Girls Club, the local YMCA, Boy Scouts, Girl Scouts or Habitat for Humanity. Check which options for networking are available in your community.

When networking, introduce yourself and hand out your business cards. Not only does it afford you the opportunity to reinforce your brand and be more memorable to those you meet, it gives them your contact information.

3. Don't be a secret agent

There was a popular television show during the 1960s called "The Beverly Hillbillies." One of the characters, Jethro Bodine, considered himself smart because he had "done graduated fifth grade." In one of the episodes, he decided to give up his dream of becoming a brain surgeon and, instead, become a "double naught" spy (like James Bond.) He converted their old farm truck into a spy vehicle and wore all sorts of disguises to blend in and maintain a low profile. It made for a great television show, but not a good idea if you are in real estate. Don't be a secret agent. Instead, make sure that *everyone* knows what you do for a living when they see you. Dress for success. Wear a smile, be approachable, and wear your name badge proudly. If you're not the name badge type, wear a monogrammed shirt or jacket with your real estate firm clearly visible. It's a great conversation starter.

I was standing in the checkout line of the local grocery, and the lady in front of me saw my name badge and started a conversation. "Oh, you're a real estate agent?" she said. "Why, yes, I am!" I replied. She immediately shared that her husband was being transferred, and they needed to sell their house. She didn't know any agents in the area. Would I be interested in helping them? Within a few days, I had listed their home, held an open house, and it soon sold and closed the same month. I got an immediate referral and listed their neighbor's home for sale. Wearing my $12 name badge had opened the door to a conversation that generated over $12,000 in business, and the conversation would never have taken place without the name badge. If you don't have your name badge on, have your radar up and look for opportunities to find clients wherever you can.

Another time, I was buying a closing gift for a special couple. I found a beautiful *Welcome Home* sign and took it to the checkout. As the clerk and I conversed at the register, she commented how lovely the sign was, and I volunteered it was for two of my favorite clients who I had helped buy their first home. She told me she was tired of paying rent and really wanted to buy a home, and asked, "Could you help me?" Within a couple of months, we had found her new home, and I was buying *her* a closing gift! Although I didn't have my badge on the day we met, I had my radar on. I made sure she knew I was in real estate and it paid off.

Always be looking and listening for opportunities to let people know that you would love to help them with their real estate needs and train your sphere of influence to have their radar up also. The next time they overhear someone talking about buying or selling a home, tell them to tackle that person by the ankles and say, "I know just who you need to call."

Make it easy for leads to come to you. Volunteer for floor duty at your office if your brokerage offers this opportunity. You will get to take the calls that come into the office and any walk-ins that are not already working with an agent. The best days for walk-ins are usually Fridays and Mondays.

4. Host open houses (OH)

Some agents don't like holding open houses. They think it's a waste of time. Perhaps, they don't understand the objective. It's two-fold. One, during the open house the agent gains leads, and qualified buyers and sellers will come to look; two, the open house will gain added exposure for the seller's home.

Because you rarely sell the home during the actual event, most listing agents will allow another agent to host an open house for them. Generally, the host will be allowed to keep all the leads, that is the names and contact information of the people who come through the open house. These are great leads. One well-planned open house can net three or more pieces of immediate business.

Holding open houses is one of the best lead generation activities an agent can do. I was in Nashville visiting my aunt, and as a new agent, I was excited about seeing and touring through every home I possibly could that was for sale. A newly renovated home was on the same street as my aunt's house, and I noticed it was listed by an out-of-area realtor whose office was over 45 minutes away. I called the listing agent and scheduled an appointment to "preview" because I didn't have a client at the time and just wanted to see the home myself.

The house was gorgeous, an absolute beauty, a winning renovation with impressive design and workmanship. I called the listing agent very eager to give her my feedback and share what a beautiful home it was. I couldn't believe the home was still available. She expressed the same disbelief and regret that she and her husband had chosen such costly renovations, thinking it would sell right away. They now sat at 180 days on the market in a market where 21 days was the norm. I asked if she had held an open house, and she said she lived too far away and didn't have the time or energy, although she knew she needed to do something. I immediately offered to hold an open house for her. She agreed. The home sold during the open house, the buyers listed their current home with me, and another prospective buyer who had missed out on that home hired me to find one like it in the area, which I did.

As a new agent, I netted a sale, a seller, and another buyer at this open house. How did this happen? It wasn't by accident. I worked very hard promoting the open house, using it as a lead generation tool. I placed three signs in the yard to advertise it as open and had the agent mark it open on the MLS (multiple listings service). I put out 10 directional pointers. You may think that's overkill, but it made a huge statement. My real estate signs were everywhere! I hung helium balloons on the mailbox, on the open house sign in the yard, and on all ten directional pointers. I posted it on social media, and I called friends, fellow agents, and prospects to invite them personally and tell them about the door prize give-a-way. The Friday before the open house, I knocked on the doors of 100 nearby homes and invited them to come to the open house for refreshments, to register for the door prize, and to get a free comparative market analysis for their home. It took over four hours to knock on 100 doors, but the effort was well worth it.

I studied the MLS sheet so that I would know everything there was to know about the house. I memorized the square footage, the type of heating and cooling, the age of the roof, school zones, etc. I took my laptop, a portable printer, and an internet connection and set up a mobile office during the open house so that I could look up comparative homes, prepare valuation reports, and have information on a nearby home that was higher and lower in price to show prospective buyers if they didn't like the one I was holding open.

During this open house, I had seventeen groups of people come through, twelve of them neighbors. The crowd created a sense of urgency in the prospective buyers. "This must be a hot property, and they better act immediately if they were interested."

I provided light refreshments—nothing too fancy, just bottled water and finger foods—and used decorative napkins. I added a fresh bouquet of flowers and offered a door prize to encourage the attendees to register. It was fun and netted great results, over $36,000 in commission from the $50 investment I spent making the flyers and buying the refreshments and door prize.

With this kind of result, it's no wonder some agents hold open houses as their sole source of leads. It takes hard work, and you do have to go that extra mile to make it a success. If all you do is put a sign in the yard and add balloons, you will get mediocre results. I must disclose that on occasion I have had less than stellar turnout, especially in rural areas where it's impossible to knock on doors and invite the neighbors. However, during those times, I lead generate from the house if foot traffic is slow, switching from hostess to prospecting mode. You can use the time to post the house on different social media networks, make phone calls, and email the flyer to all the agents that service the area. The open house is never a waste of time when you can reassure the sellers you spoke with "X" number of people about their home, even though the physical traffic for the open house was slow.

5. Door knocking

Door knocking is a very effective form of lead generation if you are willing to make the effort. Dress for the weather and wear comfortable shoes. Take someone with you if you can. It's safer and more enjoyable. Don't get bogged down spending hours and hours creating a professional flyer to hand out. Keep it simple. One young mom enrolled in my coaching program was struggling with balancing motherhood and being able to devote the time it took to build her real estate business. She wanted to spend time with her five-year-old daughter this weekend, but knew she had to make flyers and door knock for her upcoming open house. During our coaching session, she lamented that she didn't have time to design a professional looking flyer. We put our heads together and decided since her daughter liked to draw and color, perhaps her daughter could make the flyer and go with her to hand them out. Her daughter drew a beautiful house with wonderful stick figures representing herself and her mom. She added the words, "Hire my mommy. She's the best real estate agent ever!" They made lots of copies, stapled her business card to the flyer, and began door knocking, hand in hand. It was a win-win. She spent quality time with her daughter and they accomplished their door knocking, and it was fun! Such a simple flyer ... what a big message. And because a mom and her little girl seemed harmless, most of the people opened their doors and talked with them. Her daughter loved walking the neighborhood and handing out the flyers, and she beamed with delight each time the homeowners complimented the lovely flyer. The mom got several good leads, even listing one of the homes in the neighborhood.

A word of caution, door knocking is not allowed in all areas. Make sure you find a neighborhood that doesn't prohibit soliciting. Know what you are going to say in advance. You could explain, "This area is very popular and desirable, and you know there are some buyers that would love to have a home in this neighborhood." Ask, "Do you happen to know of anyone that has mentioned they might be ready to sell their home? Would you call me if you hear of someone?" Give them your card. You can also offer them something of value like your mobile app so they can keep up with home prices in the neighborhood. If your firm does not supply a mobile app for you, there are several available that can be branded back to you so that it captures leads for you.

You may have to knock on 50 to 100 doors to get one or two good leads, but if you get a listing, remember, you'll usually get three to four more pieces of business from people calling about the listing.

6. Prospecting "For Sale by Owners"

"For Sale by Owner" is one of my favorite sources of lead generation. They already want to sell their house. They just don't know they need an agent ... yet. You may think that F.S.B.O. stands for "For Sale by Owner," but it actually stands for "fastest source of business out there!" Don't try and list the home over the phone when you call an F.S.B.O. That's what the other agents do. Set yourself apart. Call them and say, "I'd like to preview your home. I understand you are probably being bombarded by agents wanting to list your home, that's not why I am calling. I just want to preview your home and see if it might be a match for some of my buyers in the future. I am already familiar with everything on the MLS and just want to personally see your home so I can describe it to my buyers in case they cannot find what they are looking for on the MLS."

First, get the appointment, get your foot in the door, get face to face with them, and then develop a connection and build that rapport. They are used to other agents being confrontational for not using an agent. You can be that agent that offers something of value. How about hosting an open house for them? After hosting one open house and doing all the work to use it as a lead generating tool as mentioned earlier in this chapter, you will be an expert. Tell them you specialize in open houses and offer this service to them. Your broker will want them to sign a form giving you permission to show the house and guaranteeing a commission in the event the home is sold during the open house or due to your efforts from the open house. Explain to the FSBO "the form doesn't establish agency, but only your compensation, should their home sell during the open house." After all, that is the plan, right?

Use the "Agreement to Show Property" form (these vary from state to state) to get a signed agreement stating what commission the seller is willing to pay should you sell their home during the open house. You supply the advertising, signage, refreshments, door-knocking, door prize, and hang the balloons on the mailbox, etc. Most "For Sale by Owners" will be excited for you to host their open house and will readily agree. If the open house goes over well and they see all the traffic your advertising and marketing efforts brought to the property, they may even list it with you. At the very least, you will pick up a buyer prospect or two.

7. Prospecting Expireds

Expireds are another good source of leads. They initially saw the value in hiring an agent to help with the sale of their home, but for some reason, their home didn't sell. Be a problem solver and help them discover why the home didn't sell. Maybe it was because they didn't hire the *right* agent! Give them a call. Sometimes you can get the phone number of the homeowner from the tax records. If not, there are paid subscriptions that offer lists with phone contacts for expireds. If you can't get the phone number, send them a letter in the mail offering to help get their home sold this time. Even the best homes don't always sell the first time around. Even better, if they reside in the home, knock on the door. There are lots of good scripts for speaking with "expireds" in the next chapter.

8. Allied Resources

Partner with your allied resources and offer to send them leads from your own customer pool. Hopefully, as they get to know you and you develop rapport, they will refer leads to you, also. Your allied resources need to be your service providers that give the best service in their field. For example, everyone will need electricians, plumbers, painters, doctors, lawyers, and barbers sooner or later, and if you are new to the area and don't have a large local sphere, use your allied resources to begin building your business contacts database.

Have you ever gone to a restaurant and received a level of service that was so over the top you wanted to tell everyone about how great the experience was? This is the type of service you are looking for in the people you recommend to your clients. Here's an exercise called the Yellow Page List. Start with the first letter in the alphabet and write a list of provider categories: accountant, architect, air conditioning technician, etc. You will need at least one name in all the categories. Go through all the letters, A to Z, writing the categories down and the names of people you know that perform that service at a high level, someone you would feel comfortable recommending. If you don't know anyone from a category, ask someone for a recommendation. Tell them you are creating a preferred vendor list and you want to know who they know that provides a 10+ level of service in that field. Get the name and contact information for the provider, tell your friend you are going to tell Joe, the plumber, that he was recommended by a raving fan. Then call Joe and have this simple conversation with him:

"Joe, this is _____, and I'm a real estate agent with _____. You don't know me, but _____ is a raving fan of yours, and they said you were their "go to" person whenever they needed a plumber. Tell me, can you take on any new clients? Great! The reason I ask is because I have clients who have just moved to the area, and they don't know who to call if they have a plumbing need. _____ says you provide a 10+ level of service, and that's the kind of service I give my clients. I only want to recommend the best, and I would love to recommend you. I'm building a list of preferred vendors to feature on my web site. May I stop by around lunch, say noon, today, for five minutes to meet you and pick up some of your business cards? I know your time is valuable and I just want to introduce myself and get those cards so I can start handing them out. Wonderful, I'll see you at noon."

This is your first touch in staying top of mind. You want them to remember you. Leave some of your business cards with them. The following week, drop by with donuts and say hello. Say that you were in the neighborhood, and you wanted to thank them for being willing to provide this service for your clients. Remind them that if they hear of anyone who needs help with real estate to keep you in mind and that you appreciate and understand how important referrals are to their business, because referrals are the lifeblood for your own business.

9. Referrals from other real estate agents

Consider these a slam dunk. When you are recommended by someone who is trusted, you would have to really mess up the appointment to not get the signed agreement. I have a fellow friend who is an agent that works onsite for a national builder. She's not allowed to sell existing homes, only those homes that the builder has in the development. Oftentimes, she has a buyer that needs to sell their current home before they can buy their new home. She refers those buyers to me. I pay her a

30% referral fee when I sell their home. She consistently sends me a listing every few months. In fact, I consider her a core advocate.

If you have moved to another state or area, you can let your sphere in your old area know you can match them with the best local realtor to help them with their real estate needs, even though you no longer live in their area. Tell them you have a network of coworkers in their area that provide a 10+ level of service so they don't end up with the wrong agent. Let them know it will help you, also, because you will receive a small referral from their brokerage commission as compensation for sending them the client.

10. Buying leads

I've never purchased leads, but some agents swear by them. Whatever side of the debate you're on, do your research. Some of the providers are all talk and no closings. Check their ratings online. Ask your fellow agents which companies offer the most successful leads and which fall short. The list of lead providers grows each day... just a few options of paid lead sources are Zillow, Trulia, Brivity, Exact Data, Realtor.com, Market Leader, Bold Leads, and RedX just to mention a few. All offer to supply you with leads for a monthly or per lead fee ranging in cost from $29 to $300 per month. Most have lengthy contracts to fulfill and it's sometimes hard to cancel your service. Read the fine print, do the research and choose carefully should this be the route you take.

Whether you choose one of the lead generation activities or all of them, the key is to be consistent. Communicate with and add 10 people to your database every day. Write letters, make the calls, meet people face to face. Remember the principle of the harvest...what activities you do today will affect your business 30 to 60 days out.

"Mules are extremely intelligent and display enhanced cognitive abilities over that of a horse or donkey. They often learn new things with as little as three repetitions."
A study of equine intelligence reported in Horse Science News Online, "Mules Smarter than Ponies," Liz Osborn

CHAPTER 4

Handling Objections with Scripts

Mules Are Quick to Learn
and Have an Excellent Memory

Once you have the leads, an important piece of the business puzzle is learning how to convert those leads into appointments, agreements, and ultimately, closings.

Although it seems like there are hundreds of different scenarios, there are only about twenty or so common objections you will hear as to why they won't sign an agreement with you on the spot. You need to be ready when these objections come up and know in advance what to say. Stammering or, even worse, not saying anything at all won't get the job done. An objection doesn't necessarily mean no, it can be a sign that they are considering hiring you. I'll hire you if...

Learning scripts is a way of preparing for these objections in advance. The desired result is to be so familiar with the script that it comes out naturally, not like the telemarketer who is reading a script. To convert more leads, you will need to learn and embed the scripts into your brain where they flow naturally as you need them. That horrible fear of rejection and being told "no" diminishes when you already know the conversation that's about to happen and you are totally prepared for it. If a mule can learn after only three repetitions, then surely, we can memorize and internalize a script. Read each script out loud three times, then practice it with a partner. With a little practice and repetition, you can learn these scripts like the back of your hand and be able to handle any objection thrown your way.

Our fears can be greatly reduced when we are ready and prepared. I like to use the example of a haunted house to illustrate. The first time you enter one of those highly popular Halloween haunted houses you are scared to death. Zombies jump out at you, evil clowns chase you, and that horrible Jason fires up the chainsaw and you run for your life. Imagine that you go through the same haunted house a second time, and a third time. Would you be as frightened the third time? Of course not, by that third time you would start to relax and enjoy yourself because now, you know what to expect. Since you know what is coming, you can respond and step out of the way just in time. Handling an objection with a script is just like the haunted house experience. The more you hear the objections and practice your response, the better you will become at handling a prospective client's objections. Once you've mastered the scripts to handle the most common objections, you will be converting more appointments into agreements, and that's a big win for you. The goal is to go on five listing appointments and get three or four to list with you instead of just converting one of those five appointments to an agreement. As you get better, it will take fewer listing appointments to get the conversions and business. That's working smarter, not harder!

Here are some of my favorite scripts to handle the most common objections. They are categorized into For Sale By Owners, Seller Objections, Buyer Objections, and Expireds. Remember a FSBO needs a problem presentation, not a listing presentation. They fully believe they can sell their home on their own without the help of an agent. So, your normal listing presentation will not work on a FSBO. They don't see the value in using an agent, in fact, they see an agent costing them money. Don't try and sell them over the phone. Ask for a preview of the home. You must win them over gradually and they will discover they have a problem selling their home without your help. You may actually save them thousands of dollars.

For Sale by Owner Scripts

Objection # 1: FSBO says, "I can sell it myself. I don't need a realtor." (Get the preview, then build a connection.)

FSBO: I've already been called by 20 other realtors, and I'm tired of telling everyone I'm not going to list my house with a realtor. I'm going to sell it myself.

Agent: I know that is aggravating! There are a lot of realtors that prospect for sale by owners to try and get you to list with them. That's not why I'm calling. I'm already familiar with every home that is on the MLS (multiple listings service), and I'd like to take a quick tour to get the feel of your home and see what it has to offer. As you know, inventory is low and my buyers can't always find the homes they want on the MLS. Seeing your home in person would allow me to describe it firsthand, and maybe your home would be the one that they've been waiting for. If I were to bring you a buyer, you would pay a buyer's commission, right? Great! I've been able to sell a lot of homes for FSBOs. I even keep an inventory notebook of homes like yours because I want to help my buyers find the home that matches their needs, even if it means taking the time to show them FSBOs. May I come by today around 5 p.m.? It will only take a few minutes. And you don't have to clean or prepare the house as if it were a normal showing. It will just be me, by myself. I won't have a client with me. Great! I'll see you at 5.

(Just get the appointment. Once you get your foot in the door, you can build the relationship and earn their trust by offering to help in ways other than listing their home. You told them over the phone that was not why you were calling, so don't ask for the listing once you get face to face with them. It will destroy any trust you build. Here's what to say when you arrive later that afternoon for your appointment.)

Agent: Mr. Jones? I'm _____ with _____ Realty. Thank you for letting me drop by on such short notice. May I come in? (Once inside, look around and find some things to compliment about the house.) You have such a beautiful home. I love the paint colors. Do you mind my asking why you are selling?"

(You are asking about their Big Why, and you need to know why they need or want to sell. They will usually volunteer that information.)

FSBO: Well, my wife is expecting another baby, and we need more room. We are just busting at the seams already, and we need a fourth bedroom.

Agent: Oh congratulations! What a joyful reason to be selling! When is the happy day? What ages are your other children? I remember when mine were around two and three, their toys took up most of our home space, and we needed a larger house, too. Tell me, have you found your next place already and are you looking locally? If you tell me a little about what you are looking for, I can keep an eye out for your next home. I look at homes every single day and sometimes run across great deals before they ever hit the market.

(Always come from contribution; offer to help them. In contrast, other agents may have been argumentative and confrontational with them because of their refusal to list the home with an agent. Don't try and change their mind or convince them they are wrong. Be helpful and congenial. Continue walking through the home and find more things to compliment in the house. Keep looking for ways to make a connection.)

Agent: I love that floor in the kitchen. Who did that for you? (If they answer they did it) Do you do this for the public? You do great work! (Notice pictures, maybe they are in the military or you can tell their occupation. Perhaps you are familiar with where their children go to school. Find as many things in common as you can. Try and find connections. As you continue through the tour, offer compliments freely and express concern at how hard it is to sell your own home and how you can appreciate what they are trying to do. After all, you do this for a living. You know how much work it is. Thank them and prepare to leave).

Agent: Will you do me a favor? If you have a prospect come through for a tour of your house and it won't work for them, would you give them one of my cards? It may turn out that I have the perfect listing for them. I'm always looking for buyers for my listings to get them sold as quickly as possible.

(Give them a stack of your cards and leave. If they have given you information as to what they want in their next house, make sure you let them know you will be in touch if you find a suitable match for their needs. Write them a thank you note for allowing you to preview the home, mail it to their address. If you have succeeded in making the connection and it went well, you will likely receive a call from them within 24 to 48 hours asking you to come back, meet their spouse, and talk with them more about selling their home. People want to do business with someone who cares, someone they feel understands their needs. You are that someone if you will take the time to connect and build the relationship. Remember, you are in the relationship business. The sale or listing is just the beginning. If you maintain the relationship, you will represent them in another sale or two and receive many referrals from them. The desired outcome is to have clients for life.)

Objection # 2: FSBO says, "I can sell it myself. I don't need a realtor." (Hiring you will make the soliciting calls from other agents stop.)

FSBO: I'm so tired of this, you are the 10th agent that's called me wanting to list my home!

Agent: I know that's aggravating, and I can make that stop for you. When you list your home with me, they will call me, not you, and that's a good plan because they will bring a buyer to get paid commission instead of just calling you to list with them.

Objection # 3: FSBO says, "I can sell it myself, I don't need a realtor." (Show them how you can actually net them more money, even after paying your commission.)

Agent: If I could show you how listing your home with me would offer a financial advantage of over 12% more profit to you, would you be interested? I can get you top dollar, expose your home through marketing to over 450 search engines, and get the job done more quickly than you can by selling it yourself. Do you have 15 minutes for me to explain how? (The National Association of Realtors did a study and discovered that 90% of FSBO's wind up selling with a realtor, and using a realtor netted the FSBO's an average of over 12% more money than selling without a realtor. Most buyers begin their search on the internet. You can get their home more exposure in the right places so that more qualified buyers can find their home).

> **Objection # 4:** FSBO says, "I can sell it myself. I don't need a realtor." (Show them they may be missing the most qualified buyers because their home is not listed on the MLS.)

Agent: Imagine for a moment that you are a buyer. If you were shopping for a home, why wouldn't you use the free service of a buyer agent? A buyer agent would search for your home, handle the negotiations, and help you navigate through all the details of the home inspection and appraisal—everything involved in the process all the way to closing—and it doesn't cost you one penny. It's been proven that most qualified buyers are working with an agent. Let me explain. There are 4 types of buyers.

The first type is the "serious and in a hurry" buyer. They are relocating and ready to buy right now. They are starting a new job or have already sold their current home and need to be settled into their new home quickly. They are prequalified and only have a short window of time to find a home before they are homeless! They are generally not going to take the time to look at *For Sale by Owner* homes, and they will call a professional agent who knows the area to help them look at the homes the agent finds for them. Most agents won't show the *For Sale by Owner* homes because they need to find a home for the buyer as quickly as possible, and they want to make sure they only show the best homes. Another reason they won't show FSBO homes is that they want to get paid for their work, and the homes on the multiple listing service offer guaranteed commissions. Your FSBO listing will be overlooked by this first type of buyer because of their urgency to find a home right away. They don't have time to drive up and down neighborhoods looking for FSBO signs.

The second type of buyer is a "needs" buyer. They need a certain type of home, something different from their current one. Maybe they are moving up in house or want some privacy or more land to go with their home or maybe they need a different school zone. They will call an agent because the agent can access the pool of other agents and the MLS and enter their specific criteria or needs to help them quickly find what they are looking for. They also need an agent to sell their current house quickly before they can buy their next one. So, you are probably not getting this second type of buyer either.

The third type of buyer is a "lowball or discount" buyer. They are investors or discount hunters who want to find a home they can buy for cents on the dollar. They will automatically back out the commission because they know you aren't paying a realtor. These buyers usually don't want to work with a professional who would understand and know the market value of property, like a real estate agent. Their main objective is to pay as little as possible, and they are successful in taking advantage of most FSBO's. You may have already gotten some lowball offers from some of these buyers.

The fourth type is what we call "pretenders or lookers." They aren't qualified and can't even buy your home. It would be horrible if you ended up getting into a contract with them. They tie up the house, sometimes even moving in before closing. Then you are in a fix because they can't get the loan to buy the house and you have squatters living in your house. An agent won't even show them a house because it's a waste of your time.

These last two types of buyers are the ones that look at FSBO's. They will slow down the process of selling your home, and the longer your home sits on the market, day after day, the more it loses value. Let me show you how I can help you sell your home for the most money in the least amount of time. I want to bring you the best buyers, not waste your time.

> **Objection # 5:** FSBO says, "I can sell it myself. I don't need a realtor." (Talk to them about all that could go wrong? An example of a problem presentation.)

Agent: Tell me, have you sold a house without an agent recently? There are a lot of problems that can arise when selling your own home even for someone who has experience. The buyers may not be qualified, and you have no way of prequalifying the prospects. You may waste time with a buyer who can't even buy the home.

Isn't your time valuable? It's terribly inconvenient to take off work to show the home, not to mention the preparation you do in getting the house ready to show. One of my FSBO friends told me he had taken off work and waited 45 minutes for a buyer. They never showed and never called back.

I hope you will be very careful, too. It's not safe for you to open the door to any stranger who happens to see the sign, pulls in the driveway, and knocks. How will you know if they are actually interested in the home or if they are up to no good? There are thieves who prey on FSBO's, pretending to be a buyer, when they only want to steal anything they can get their hands on. Once inside, they case the home, spot the items they want, and learn how the house is laid out. Then they wait and watch the homeowners leave. They can be in and out with the stolen items in a matter of minutes!

I had an FSBO call me to list their home. They were done with trying to sell it on their own. He told me a buyer had pretended to need the restroom, went through the medicine cabinet, and took his prescription pain medicine. Another FSBO had a diamond bracelet and several other valuable items stolen from the jewelry box on the dresser. Everyone who comes into your home needs to be vetted, and most FSBO's do not have a way to do that like a professional agent can. I make a copy of their driver's license, run a quick background check, and get a copy of their pre-approval letter from their lender before ever showing them a property.

It's not just safety. The home inspection process can be very costly if you don't have experience in this area.

Everyone who buys a home will want a home inspection, and I am very familiar with common issues and problems that arise. I can help my clients navigate through the inspection process, possibly saving them thousands of dollars.

Lastly, although home prices have shot up, the appraisals aren't quite coming in high enough, and sometimes they come in very low. I help my clients negotiate through a low appraisal, should that happen. No one wants the deal to fall apart from a bad appraisal.

Sticking the sign in the yard and getting a buyer is the easy part. Holding the deal together and saving my clients money all the way through closing is where they see the value of hiring me to help. Let me help you. I can take all this stress off you. Just sign me up and I'll handle all of this for you.

> **Objection # 6:** FSBO says, "Will you lower your commission?" (Explain the cost of marketing and that their house will get less exposure with a discounted broker.)

FSBO: I'll sign with you, but only if you lower your commission.

Agent: I may not be the cheapest agent, but I don't cut corners with my listings. Discount brokers seem to know what their service is worth. I'm sure you know that I operate within a certain profit level to run my business successfully. In order to do the amount of advertising that it takes to sell your home, I need to have 6% minimum commission. There may be other agents who will discount their commission and service you for less. It's because they're not marketing your home like I do. I subscribe to many search engines and offer the most exposure for your listing because that's what sells. Look at the math. At 6% commission, I offer 3% to the agent who brings a buyer.

Of my 3%, 1% goes to marketing and overhead, 1% goes to Uncle Sam. That leaves me 1% for my earnings. If I lowered my commission, the only thing I could adjust would be the amount of marketing that I do. My marketing is what makes your home sell in the shortest amount of time for the most money. We don't want to cut corners there.

> **Objection # 7:** Seller had a bad experience with a previous agent. (Explain that not all agents are alike.)

Seller: I've worked with an agent before, and I hated it. It was awful.

Agent: I'm sorry to hear that. Everyone has had a bad experience doing business. I'd love to sit down with you so you can tell me what went wrong. I want to know all about it. I specialize in selling homes that didn't sell the first time. What I offer to my clients is unique in this industry. Many agents don't listen to the seller's goals and needs. I do far more than just put the sign in the yard, place it on the MLS, and sit back and wait for a buyer to come. I proactively search for buyers every single day, and I begin the selling process with an analysis of my seller's goals so that I have a clear picture of your goal in selling your house, your time frame, and everything that's important to you about selling your house. I try and exceed the expectations my sellers and I have set. May I come by this afternoon at 4:00, or would 5:30 work better for you?

Seller Objections

Objection # 8: Seller says, "Will you lower your commission?" (Discount brokers know their value.)

Seller: I'll sign with you, but only if you lower your commission. Are you willing to list my house for 4%?

Agent: Discount brokers know their true value and they have priced at a discount because they give discount services. If they thought they could ask full price, they would, but they know they are not delivering the full package, the years of experience, the negotiating skills, and the full marketing package I'm offering. Have you ever bought something at a discount store and found out you got what you paid for? Don't risk one of your largest investments to a discount broker.

Objection # 9: Seller says, "Will you lower your commission?" (If an agent is too quick to lower their commission)

Seller: Joe from ReFax said he would sell my home for 5%. Will you sell it for 5%?

Agent: Wow, Joe said that? How much negotiating did you do before he was willing to give up 1% of his commission?

Seller: I didn't have to. He offered it up front!

Agent: Really? You know what scares me about that? Joe's idea of negotiating is lowering the price to get the listing. Look how quickly he gave up his own money. How strong a negotiator will he be when it's *your* money? You need a strong agent who is an experienced negotiator and will fight for every dollar of your money! Don't you think you'd be better off with an agent like me than with an agent whose first negotiation tactic is lowering the price?

> **Objection # 10:** Seller says, "You are a new agent. I want someone with more experience." (Hiring you doesn't means less service or knowledge)

Seller: You are new, right? I think I would feel better hiring someone with a little more experience.

Agent: Yes, I'm new, but rest assured that *because* I'm new I have intentionally aligned myself with a team of experienced agents. My clients will get the benefit of my passion and fresh approach in addition to getting the experience and wisdom of the seasoned agents working alongside of me. And getting your home sold will be our number one priority. You won't be just a number in a crowd like you would be if using a more experienced agent on a big team. No one will work harder for you than I will to get your home sold. I can devote all my attention to exactly what needs to be done to sell your home for the most money in the shortest amount of time.

> **Objection # 11:** Seller says, "I want to price my home higher." (Another agent says it's worth more just to get the listing.)

Seller: Sue at ABC Realty says I can price my home much higher if I list with her. I want the most money I can get. I feel like you don't think my house is worth as much as Sue does.

Agent: You've seen the comps. We've looked at them together. It's not about opinions. It's the market that determines the value of your home. I don't want to get your hopes up or mislead you into thinking you can get way above market value. That's not in your best interest. You do want to get top dollar for your home, I understand. If your price is over the market value, it will just sit there without selling, being passed over. The longer your home sits on the market the more the value will go down. In a hot market like we are in, if a house sits on the market more than a few weeks, the buyers start thinking there is something wrong with the house and they pass it over. I've seen it happen over and over to overpriced homes.

A few agents may not be familiar with the market. Or, it might be that they may encourage you to list at a higher price because that's what you want to hear, and it gets them the listing. Once they get their sign in your yard, it's a win for them. But not so much for you. Their sign works like a billboard advertisement for them. They get lots of calls from buyers inquiring about your home, and because it is priced too high, the agent can steer them to another home, something more reasonably priced in accordance with the market. They end up selling the other home instead of yours because yours is the bait for getting them more business. In the meantime, their sign in your yard keeps attracting more buyers for other homes. The longer their sign stays in your yard, the better it is for them. That's not how I operate. I want to get you top dollar and get your home sold in the shortest amount of time so that you can get the children settled in your new home before school starts. That's my priority! I'm not interested in using your home to sell other houses, I'm interested in getting YOUR home sold, first and foremost. Does Sue know how important your timeline of getting your kids settled in your new house is to you? Now, who do you think really has *your* best interests in mind?

> **Objection # 12:** Seller says, "I want to price my home higher." (Leaving wriggle room for negotiating is a bad idea.)

Seller: I want to price my home about $10,000 to $15,000 higher so I'll have a cushion for negotiating.

Agent: Okay, let's talk about that. We used to recommend doing that because in a normal market, that would make sense. Not anymore. We are in a seller's market, and we have more buyers than homes right now! The cushion room pricing technique backfires on us in this market. Have you ever been to an auction? If more than one person wants the same item, what happens to the price? It goes up. They bid against each other. Homes are like that. If we price your home at market value, chances are good that more than one buyer will be attracted at the same time, and we could end up getting more than the asking price for your home, ending up with multiple offers. However, if we price your home above the market value, we will lose about 90% of prospective buyers, and maybe only one buyer will make an offer. And if we only have one offer, that leads to negotiating, and the price usually gets negotiated down. Now which tactic do you think will net you the most money in the end? Exactly, let's price it at market and get you the most money in the shortest amount of time.

> **Objection # 13:** Seller says, "I want to price my home higher." (I can drop the price later if it doesn't sell is not a good plan.)

Seller: If it doesn't sell, we can always drop the price next month.

Agent: Yes, we can always go down on the price, but timing is everything. That might be too little, too late! We will attract the most qualified buyers in the first few days and weeks of your listing. There's an urgency for the buyers to make a quick offer on just listed homes so that it doesn't get away. Remember, we are in a hot market, and homes are moving quickly. So, in everyone's mind, your home should move quickly, too. Have you ever seen a home for sale that you know has been for sale for months? You think something must be wrong with that home because it's been on the market a long time. If you ever were interested in that house, you'd make a low offer because of the extended days on the market. Most buyers would think the sellers are desperate and panicking, wanting to get the home sold, so they will make a much lower offer. I know you're not desperate, but the longer your home stays on the market, the more the price will need to drop to get it sold. I've seen buyers fall in love with a home and want to make an offer, but the price is so much out of the market the buyers don't even make the offer for fear of insulting the seller! Let's price it at market and attract the best buyers from the very beginning. We don't want those best buyers to pass us over and buy a different home. We want them to buy yours!

> **Objection # 14:** Seller says, "I don't want to put my home on the market until I find the home I want to buy." (Seller doesn't want to be homeless.)

Seller: We know we want to sell, but I want to find the home we want to buy and get it under contract before I list my home.

Agent: Yes, that would be ideal, and lots of sellers do this. Let me ask you a question. Let's say we list your home, and you get two offers. The first offer is almost full price, and the buyer can close in 30 days. The second offer is for more than asking price; however, they want you to wait for them to sell their house and take your home off the market while they try and sell theirs. They've got a closing possibly out 60 to 90 days, that is, if their home sells. If it doesn't, you would need to give them their earnest money back and start all over. Which offer would you pick? Most sellers would pick the lower offer and not wait on an "if" buyer that needs to sell their home first.

This scenario of finding a house first and then listing your home for sale is a lose/lose for you unless you are financially able to buy the next house without selling your current home. If not, chances are you will find a fabulous home you can't live without, and you'll end up making an offer well over the asking price because you want them to wait while you sell your home. Then you'll price your current home well under what you hoped to get for it because now, you must sell it fast! You lose both ways. Now, if we price your home to sell at market value and get it under contract, then you are a stronger buyer. You have a closing date and a stronger case to assure the seller you will be able to buy their home. I understand you want to know you will be able to find just the right home before selling this one. I just don't want you to fall in love with one too soon and lose money on both the buying and selling side! Let's get your home listed and ready to sell and get you a buyer so you can find your next home. That way, if your home is already under contract or even better, closed, you will be a much stronger buyer and get a better deal on your next home. Some sellers intentionally close before they have their next home and then will rent so they can take their time looking and not feel panicked or pressed for time to jump into just any home. They can look until they find that perfect one, and when they do, they have their money and are ready to go and move to the top of the list of offers, being one of those strong buyers, the kind sellers want. Does that make sense?

Objection # 15: Seller says, "I want to sell the house as is." (Seller doesn't want to fix it up before selling it.)

Seller: I don't have the time or energy to remodel the house, repaint everything, and stage it. Can't I just sell it "as is"?

Agent: Well, you could, however it would affect the price you ultimately get for your home and how many days it stays on the market. Let me explain. There are four reasons why a home doesn't sell: price, location, condition, and presentation. Three of these we can control. The location, well, unless you are going to jack up the house and move it, you can't control the location. Even though it's a seller's market, buyers are still looking for a home in good condition. Put yourself in their shoes. Would you want to have to entirely paint a home, lay new flooring, and wait for a couple of weeks after buying it before you could move in? And your competition knows this and will have their home in the best condition possible. If condition is an obstacle in the buyer's mind, then the only solution is to get the home at a lower price. Are you willing to price your home well below market value just to avoid the pain of having to improve the condition? I know several painters who could make your home look like new for a very reasonable cost, especially in comparison with the value it will add and the shortened time on the market. Painting and making everything fresh more than pays for itself in the long run. Let's call them and get started. It really does make a difference to the buyers. You want your home to sell sooner than later, right?

> **Objection # 16:** You can tell your appointment went well and you've connected and you're ready to sign the paperwork, then the seller says… "I'm going to interview three agents before I decide." (They read somewhere that they were supposed to interview more than one agent.)

Seller: I'm going to talk with three agents. I don't want to just hire the first agent I speak with because I want to make sure I hire the right one. I'm not signing anything today until I finish the interviewing process.

Agent: A lot of my clients do that also. Tell me, after we've met today and you've seen all the information I've shared with you, other than wanting to finish the interviews, is there any other reason why you would not hire me today? No? Perfect. Well, why not get started marketing your home immediately instead of spending several more days and possibly losing the buyers that are looking this very weekend? I know you probably feel obligated to hold the interviews since they are already scheduled, and they are going to spend a lot of preparation time getting ready for the interview. Why not allow me to call them and tell them I convinced you to go ahead and hire me today? It will save them all that time in preparation, and they could be spending that time with their families. I can tell them that because they were your next choice, you wanted them to have the first opportunity to show the house before the listing goes live on the MLS. Let's sign the paperwork and get started right now. I can make those calls for you to the other agents. I've done it before many times.

Expired Objection

> **Objection # 17:** Seller says, "I'm going to relist with the same agent." (The seller is comfortable with their old agent and doesn't want to change.)

Seller: I'm probably going to use the same agent I used last time.

Agent: Let me ask you something. Do you think your agent did the best they possibly could to sell your house this last time? Of course, you do, or you wouldn't be thinking of relisting with him. He listed it on the multiple listings service, advertised it, held it open, networked with his resources, and hoped to get a buyer. The problem is that he still has the same source of buyers that he had last time. I have a totally different source of buyers that haven't seen or heard about your home yet. Doesn't it make more sense to list with me and allow me to offer it to thousands of new buyer prospects instead of offering it to the same buyers again? Let me sell your home, I can get this done for you!

> **Objection # 18:** Expired Seller says, "It was listed before, why didn't you bring a buyer then?" (Seller thinks that when it was listed before you should have seen it and sold it then.)

Seller: If you are so good at selling homes, why didn't you sell it when it was listed before?

Agent: That's a fair question, and I can answer that. You see, you need to sell a home twice to actually get it sold. First, you need to sell it to all the other agents. They need to feel like the home is a great prospect for their buyers, priced right, and in good condition. Once you've sold it to the agents, they'll bring their buyers, and the buyers will make the offers. May I be frank with you? Your previous agent didn't sell it to me. I saw the listing, but the presentation just didn't impress me that this home was right for my buyers. And that first look is the most important one. The online presence makes or breaks the interest in your home. Let me show you how I would showcase your home and attract other agents to bring their buyers.

Buyer Objections

Objection #19: Buyer won't sign an agency agreement. (Buyer wants to self-shop for best deal and not commit to one agent.)

Buyer: I want to be free to work with other agents and look for my home myself. I don't want to sign a buyer's agreement to work with just one agent.

Agent: I understand. However, working with me doesn't prevent you from looking on your own. I will be sending you several of my resources for finding homes that are great tools. Keep in mind that we are in a fast market, and a lot of the homes go under contract almost immediately and will no longer be available. And this information is only available to a licensed agent. I only work with buyers who are willing to work with me exclusively. I provide a service for my clients that includes hours and hours of searching for their property, preparing market analysis to assist them in pricing and prevent them from overpaying for their new home. I'll be networking with other agents to find homes even before they hit the market. I'll be negotiating on my clients' behalf to get them the most home for the money, then negotiating through their home inspection and appraisal process to make sure their purchase stays on track and goes as smoothly as possible. All I ask is that if you visit an open house, a new construction model, or a *For Sale by Owner* that you tell them you are working with me. It doesn't cost you one penny to use my services, and you have everything to gain. The seller pays my commission. You can see that because of the amount of time I spend working for my buyers exclusively, I need them to work with me exclusively, also. The buyer's agreement just says that you are giving me permission to represent you in a real estate transaction so that the seller can pay me at closing.

> **Objection 20:** Buyer wants to offer much less than asking price. (Buyer wants to wheel and deal and offer 50 cents on the dollar.)

Buyer: I know the home is listed at $200,000, but I want to offer $150,000 and see what happens.

Agent: Other than not wanting to pay full price, do you think the home is worth $200,000 to other buyers? Yes? Well then, let's talk about strategy. The market says the home is worth $200,000, and you agree it's not overpriced. So, the seller would be giving away $50,000 of his equity to sell it at that price. Let me ask you a question. If the seller counters back, would you be willing to go up in price? How much? Well, the reason I ask is because this price range is one of the fastest selling ranges on the market. It's very affordable as a first-time home purchase or investment, and the seller knows this. What if, while you were making your low offer, another buyer came in and offered full price? Would you be upset if this one got away? You would?

Then let's be strategic and show the seller you are a qualified and knowledgeable buyer, willing to make a reasonable offer on his home. That's a better strategy than wasting time and possibly losing this home, or worse, making the seller angry so that he doesn't even counter. If you really want to buy this home, let's make a good offer. Of course, I am bound to follow your instructions if you insist on making that low offer; however, I highly advise against it. It could backfire on you and cost you a great house.

> **Objection # 21:** Buyer wants to see everything that's on the market. (Buyer doesn't want to miss that perfect one if it's out there.)

Buyer: I want to be sure I don't miss that perfect house.

Agent: Usually, my buyers can find their next home in the first 12 homes I show them. If you're good at telling me what you want and need and if I'm good at listening, we should be able to find your home right away. Don't be surprised if the very first one we look at turns out to be the one you want to buy.

(Tip: Always show the best home first. Don't save the best for last. Saving the best for last makes the buyer feel that the homes are getting a little bit better with each new showing, so they think the next home will be a better one. If you show the best first, then everything else drops off, and the choice is easier.)

There are scripts for every occasion that can be found online. Remember, if you want to sell like a mule you have to be quick on your feet. A mule can learn with only 3 repetitions. Practice your responses to the most common objections, and your confidence will soar through the roof. You will be ready for any obstacle thrown your way, and you will see your appointment to agreement conversions increase exponentially.

"Mules are dainty steppers and take small, sure footed steps, a quality that is immensely useful in rough terrains. In addition to small steps, they put their rear foot in exactly the same spot where their front foot has been. This leaves very little room for slipping errors." Excerpt from National Geographic Visitor Center, Grand Canyon Blog, "Mules Reign Supreme Over Horses in the Grand Canyon." July 16, 2012, Author Unknown

CHAPTER 5

Know Your Contracts
Mules Are Careful and Sure Footed

As an agent, it is your fiduciary duty to know and understand contracts. Anything less is considered negligence and could result in the loss of your license. In the real estate world where hundreds of thousands of dollars are at stake, ignorance is not an excuse. Not only do you need to know how to correctly fill out an agreement, you need to know how to explain to the client what they are signing and that it is a legal document that creates certain rights and obligations.

The application of contract knowledge is an area where both new and seasoned agents can excel ... or fail miserably. As a principal broker for over 300 agents, I had the opportunity to look at thousands of contracts as they came across my desk for review. By simply scanning how the contract was filled out, I could discern within a matter of seconds whether the agent had knowledge and experience or were novices. Especially if there were blank spaces or information filled in the wrong spaces. Just like me, the cooperative agent (the agent on the other side of the transaction) is making a judgment call on your knowledge and expertise based on how you have filled out the contract. If the contract is well constructed and iron clad, offering all areas of protection for your client and written within the premise that you are well versed in current market trend, the impression you leave will be one of a strong agent who is knowledgeable in your field, with experience where it matters. This sets the expectation that the offer is fair and acceptable to their client. With this impression, the negotiation process immediately tips to your advantage.

In contrast, a poorly written offer leaves the impression that you don't know what you are doing or that you are new and inexperienced, tipping the negotiation process to their advantage.

Contracts vary from state to state and even from brokerage to brokerage. Most of the commonly used contracts for residential sales have been created by state attorneys representing the local real estate associations. In Tennessee, these forms are called TAR (Tennessee Association of Realtors) forms and are copyrighted for use by registered members only. When the forms are pulled from the state website source, the name of the agent requesting to use the form is automatically imprinted at the bottom of each page. Agents may use the forms once they become members of their local association of realtors, which gives them membership to their local board, statewide board, and the nationally recognized board (NAR or National Association of Realtors).

All Realtors are expected to follow ethical guidelines as laid out by the NAR rules and regulations, and members must complete an ethics class every two years to stay in membership. As a real estate agent, you cannot give these forms to a *For Sale by Owner* unless you are representing one of the parties in the transaction. Some states allow exceptions and will permit the agent to offer specific state required condition disclosures to an unrepresented party. Always check with your local board and broker to see what regulations apply in your state. The state forms are copyrighted, which means the wording is intentional and the agent using the form should not change or strike through the wording in any way. In fact, your error and omission insurance may not protect you in the event you change the wording or use an expired or outdated form. Never strike through; it is a better practice to use an addendum or amendment to the agreement to address any changes needed.

Using standardized state forms are not mandatory in every instance. However, using them lowers your liability because they offer a wider area of protection for you, your client, your brokerage and all parties involved in the transaction. Remember, licensed real estate attorneys have created these contracts so trust your mule, even though you've never met...they know what they are doing.

There are some exceptions. Some brokerages and other entities may choose to create their own contract forms. Most new construction builders prefer their own customized forms. This is acceptable provided they offer the protection needed for you and your client, and most do. When using a non-traditional contract, check with your broker if you have specific questions about liability and protection for you, your brokerage, and the client.

In truth, a real estate contract can be handwritten on a brown paper bag while leaning on the hood of your car. I am witness to this. Although legal, it is certainly not the best option. The contracts created by the state attorneys are uniform and are divided into standard sections that address the different terms, rights, and obligations of the parties involved. These state contracts are updated every year by real estate attorneys. A committee of agents will meet to discuss the issues that have emerged over the past year and, under the guidance of the attorneys, revise the contracts as needed.

In 2008 when the real estate market crashed, we began seeing more short sales, foreclosures, and issues dealing with third party approvals, which caused chaos and abnormalities. For the first time we saw problems arising from extended closing dates, required third party approval, and second and third mortgages needing to be addressed. Imagine the logistical problems when a binding agreement was reached, and a third party (the creditor or lender) was required to approve the terms of the sale before it could go forward. Keep in mind that the buyer had specific performance deadlines and these were being performed before learning if the offer would even be accepted by the lender. Buyers were paying for $500 appraisals and $500 home inspections, and then the terms might be rejected by the third party ... sometimes 90 days later.

Another flourish of changes or revisions to the contracts came after the great flood of 2010 in Nashville, Tennessee. The intrusive water covered Opryland Hotel, causing millions of dollars in damage. Flood plains had to be redrawn and addressed in more detail. There was an increase in sink holes because of the flooding and a provision for reporting those were added. Every state has different issues and updates are made annually and the newly revised contracts go into effect January of each year.

The changes are posted on the state association site where the forms can be downloaded. Each year, your brokerage will expect you to attend a contract class taught by your principal broker that addresses any changes or additions to the contracts.

If you are a new agent, your principal broker will also require you to attend basic contract training within the first six weeks of obtaining your license. It's your broker's responsibility to ensure that you are well versed in writing and understanding contracts. After all, they are liable for your mistakes and for every agreement you write. The most common transactions include representing a client to buy, sell, or lease a home or land, and listing a home for sale. You should be familiar with the contracts needed for these basic transactions.

Let's examine the process of a residential purchase and sale. Working with a buyer will most likely be your first transaction. We will begin with the contracts and paperwork involved with representing a buyer in a purchase.

In Tennessee, as in most states, agency is not inferred. To establish agency, you must have a written agreement with your buyer hiring you to represent them in the transaction. The Confirmation of Agency does not create agency, it only confirms or clarifies who is representing whom. Agency is one of the most misunderstood concepts in real estate transactions. It is the most frequent source of complaints where agents get into serious trouble with their real estate commission. In a perfect world, you will only represent one party in each transaction.

One of the first contracts or forms you will need signed is the Buyer's Representation Agreement. This clearly establishes that you are entitled to be paid a commission when your client closes on their home. I work as a Designated Agent for the Buyer so that I am the only agent within my company who is representing the buyer. The principal broker has designated one agent to represent the buyer. In contrast, Agent for the Buyer creates an agency with the entire firm, making every agent within the company also a representative for the buyer.

This could accidentally cause dual agency or representing both the buyer and the seller in the same transaction. You can easily see how this could create a conflict of interest and result in misunderstandings and claims of unfair practices which could lead to a complaint against the agent and brokerage.

Although it is best to represent only one party in the transaction, the lure of receiving both the buyer's and seller's commission plus a pre-existing relationship with both parties can cause agents to "double dip." You still want to avoid dual agency (representing both clients against each other in a transaction), so here are some options that will help protect everyone if you are writing the offer on a listing where you are already representing the seller.

Option 1. Agents may represent one party and allow the other party to proceed without representation. You are already the listing agent, and a buyer comes to your open house or calls you from the sign and wants to write an offer on your listing. Great care must be taken to make certain everyone in the transaction is clear as to who is representing whom. There are specific forms that need to be signed by all parties when an unrepresented buyer is involved in the transaction. I recommend explaining to the buyer that you represent the seller so they should not tell you how high they are willing to go if their initial offer is only the beginning offer. Explain that you are required to disclose to the seller any information that would give the seller an advantage, so they should exercise caution so as not to show their "poker hand." If they feel comfortable proceeding, and you are certain they are well versed in what is customary, and you make sure all opportunities for protection as a consumer are in place for them (home inspection, contingent upon financing, etc.), then you can write the offer for the unrepresented buyer. The Confirmation of Agency will need to clearly show that you represent the seller and the buyer is making the offer unrepresented. The buyer will also need to sign additional forms explaining they understand their options and have clarity on how agency works.

Option 2. Sometimes an agent who has the listing will change their representation from Designated Agent for the Seller to Facilitator. In this role, the agent is a neutral party and cannot disclose information to either the buyer or seller that would offer an advantage. They can help both the buyer and seller and make sure the terms and conditions are clearly written and understood, but they may not advise either party as to the price or other terms and conditions. They only facilitate. In both options (Option 1 Unrepresented Buyer and Option 2 Facilitator), the agent is entitled to the full listing commission, both the commission for the selling side and the buying side.

In a normal transaction where you are only representing one party, let's assume you are representing the buyer and you are not the listing agent. I use the Buyer's Representation Agreement that the buyer will need to sign as my interview sheet as I am doing the buyer's consultation. Although the forms may vary from state to state, there are blanks to fill in, and using the form as your interview sheet prompts you to ask detailed questions about what type of residence the buyer is looking for, price range, number of bedrooms, areas, school zones, and more. After you have filled out the form, explain that you will be working exclusively with them as their Designated Buyer Agent, if that is what your brokerage practices, to help them find their perfect home. That means that if another buyer you are representing wants the exact same home they are considering, you promise not to work against them. Anything else is a conflict of interest, and you are not performing your fiduciary duty and placing their needs first.

If two of your buyers want the same property, you will need to refer one buyer to another agent for at least that one transaction. In exchange for your loyalty and all the time and effort you will be expending in the search for their home, ask for their loyalty as well. "Mr. Buyer, I know you are excited about finding your new home, and all I ask is that if you visit an open house or stop by a new construction model or visit a *For Sale by Owner* property, you immediately let them know I am representing you. Give them one of my cards. If you don't let them know I am representing you, then I won't be able to negotiate on your behalf should that home be the one you decide to buy. I want to help protect your interests, make sure that you get the best house for your money, and make sure you don't get taken advantage of. Sound okay?" Then I ask for them to sign the Buyer's Representation Agreement. Most states do not have inferred agency relationships. Even so, it's best to have agreements establishing agency in writing.

Now that you have agency addressed and you have found that perfect home for your client, you will need a Purchase and Sale Agreement. In this agreement, you will clearly spell out the terms of the agreement. In addition to the price being offered, there are many other terms to be negotiated. Will your buyer need financing? How much money are they able to put down? How much time will their lender need to complete the loan? Who will their lender be? How much trust or earnest money can they pay up front to show they are vested in the property? Do they want a home inspection? Do they want or need an appraisal? When do they want to close? When do they want possession? Do they want a home warranty? Are there any special requests that are important to the buyer in order to complete the transaction? All of these items fall under the definition of "terms" of the contract. Most purchase and sale agreements are several pages in length and divided into sections. Become familiar with your forms, and ask your broker for help if you have questions when filling them out.

In addition to the Buyer Representation Agreement and the Purchase and Sale Agreement, you will need other forms to complete the transaction. For example, if the house was built before 1978, you will need to use the Lead Based Paint Disclosure form supplied by your state. Most of the additional forms needed for a transaction will be initiated by the seller because they are required to provide them to the buyer, so don't start it from a blank. Instead, ask the seller's agent to provide the seller-initiated forms to you and then have your buyer finish their portion and sign it.

A Property Condition Disclosure is usually required. In Tennessee, as well as in many other states, there are three types of disclosures. If the seller has lived in the house for even one day during the last three years, he/she is required to fill out the full Property Condition Disclosure. This form consists of several pages and requires the seller to list every major item in the home that conveys at no additional cost and to disclose if any of the items are defective or in non-working order. A second disclosure is the Exemption Disclosure. If the owner has not lived in the home in the last three years, he can fill out the shorter Exemption Disclosure because he is not expected to know what is working or not working in the home. If you inherit a home, you can use this form, or a landlord who has not lived in the home can use the exemption. A third property disclosure is the Disclaimer. This is commonly used for bank owned homes and auctions where the home is being sold as is with no liability or responsibility of the seller to fill out a Property Condition Disclosure.

Your brokerage may have other forms such as a mold or radon disclosure that they require. In most states, whether representing a buyer or a seller, the brokerage is required to disclose affiliations or business interest with cooperative vendors such as mortgage companies and title companies if any money has been paid such as rent for an office or advertising sponsorships, especially if any parties to the transaction might be using one of those vendors.

Timelines and deadlines are built into every agreement. It is not a legal contract unless it has a starting time and an expiration time. Make sure you note all the timelines and dates for performance. Missing a performance deadline, such as completing a home inspection, can cause your client to accept the home "as is," even if severe defects were found during the home inspection that would have given your client the right to terminate the contract had the inspection been performed on time. It is your responsibility to make sure all timelines are met and that your client has total clarity of when these timelines are due and what performance is expected. Timelines and terms will be discussed in greater detail in the next chapter, "Working with Buyers."

We've talked about the forms needed when representing buyers; now let's look at the forms needed when representing a seller. Instead of the Buyer's Representation Agreement, you will use something like the Exclusive Right to Sell form. Again, we practice Designated Agency so that only one agent is representing the seller. This form creates the "listing" and spells out not only all the details of what is included, but the timeline for accomplishing the sale and how much commission is offered to the brokerage when the sale is complete. You will want to consider that whatever commission you quote will be

SELL LIKE A MULE

cut in half. For example, if you list the home for 6%, you will most likely share half of it, 3%, with the buyer agent that brings the buyer. The commission is offered by the listing firm on the Multiple Listing Service and is separate from the transaction and never negotiated as part of the buyer's offer.

Other forms commonly used for listing a home are the Confirmation of Agency (which confirms who is representing whom) and the Property Condition Disclosure (whichever of the three disclosures apply). Have the seller fill out the Property Condition Disclosure. Do not fill it out for him. It is okay to assist with questions the seller may have, but it is best to allow the seller to answer the questions to the best of their ability because this will protect them in a court of law should litigation over condition arise. If the house is older than 1978, you will need the seller to fill out the Lead Based Paint Disclosure. Some firms use a brokerage disclaimer agreement that indemnifies the firm if an agent were to claim an area of expertise where there was none. For example, if an agent were to say, "Why, this house has a great roof on it. I climbed up there myself, and it looks fine." Unless the agent is a licensed roofer, he should not make a claim about the roof's condition. The brokerage disclaimer form usually consists of all the areas the agent claims to have no area of expertise in and states that he is only representing the consumer for real estate purposes.

Your brokerage may have a few other specific forms they require for listings. Always ask your broker what is customary.

Whatever forms you use, it is imperative to leave a copy of the signed forms with your client immediately after they have been signed, or "executed." Either take spare forms and fill out two copies, or if signing the forms digitally, immediately share a copy of the forms to their email once they are signed and completed.

There are two types of signatures your client can use to execute a form: 1) digital and 2) wet sign. Digital signatures are available over secure software programs that your brokerage will offer. They are acceptable in almost all cases. It is best for each party that is signing to have their own email address, instead of a husband and wife sharing the same email.

Wet sign is using pen and ink to sign on paper in person. In some instances, this is preferred. Certain government paperwork and currently all closing documents must be wet signed. Digital signatures for closings are not yet universally recognized although probably will be in the future.

Remember, one of your most important values as an agent is the ability to protect your client and construct a well-written agreement. Study diligently and become a contract master. Double check your agreements for errors and have your client double check them also. Immediately provide copies of all executed (signed) contracts to your client and firm. We will cover more about the listing contract timelines and procedures in the upcoming chapter, "Working with Sellers."

Be careful and thoughtful when writing and responding to contracts. Be safe, take initiative and think like a mule. Know your contracts...put the rear foot exactly where the front foot has stepped so there is little chance for error.

"Compared to its parents, a mule shows much more reasonable thinking with curiosity, with a good sense of self-preservation, and often it has been noted that it does not lead its rider forward if it senses danger." *Interestingfunfacts.com, May 3, 2012, "Information about Mules."* Author unknown.

CHAPTER 6

Working with Buyers

Conduct a Great Interview...
A Mule Comes from Curiosity

Buyers are fun to work with. They are usually happy, excited, and looking forward to the opportunity of previewing houses and picking out their next home. Working with a buyer is often your first transaction. The lead will most likely come from a close family member or friend.

Get to know your buyer by conducting a great interview. It is best to meet the prospective buyer at your office instead of at the property, especially if you've never met before. If you don't have an office, use the conference room at your brokerage or meet them in a safe place that is public, like a quiet restaurant or community meeting room. This provides for a better experience and less distraction so you can thoroughly assess your buyer's needs.

Using the D.I.S.C. information from Chapter 2, identify their most dominant personality style, and adjust your conversation to their preferred way of communicating. Ask relevant questions and take notes. Use your Buyer's Representation Agreement Form as a guide and write your notes on it as you are interviewing the buyer. Some of the questions you will want to ask are: Why are you buying? How soon will you need to be in your new home? What is on your list of needs and wants?

Continue with who will be living in the home, if school zones are important, are pets a factor, what location will the buyers need, and clarify the daily commute. Another important question is which lender will be writing their preapproval letter if they are financing the purchase. Explain to them that in a hot market the sellers want the preapproval letter submitted at the same time as the offer. Instead of asking, "Are you preapproved?" Phrase your question in the following manner, "Go ahead and give me the name and contact information of the lender you will be using so that I can get the preapproval letter to submit with the offer when we find your perfect home." This seems less offensive to buyers. If their response is, "Well, we haven't quite gotten that far yet. We haven't spoken with a lender or decided on one yet." Your reply should be, "Well, I can help you with that, too. I've kept a list of the lenders that my clients have loved working with. Let me give you this lender's contact information. He can help you get preapproved and find out exactly what type of monthly payment you feel comfortable with so that we know the correct price range to be looking in. Here's his information. Let's call him before we actually look at any homes, and he can answer your questions and get you preapproved, usually within a matter of hours."

As their agent, you will want to know that they are financially qualified to buy. You don't want to waste your time showing them houses day after day, week after week, and then write an offer only to find out they can't even buy a home because of credit issues. If financing is required, the first order of business should be loan preapproval.

Interest rates are based on the customer's credit worthiness in addition to the federal rate. Some consumers get lower rates than others do because of excellent credit and assets.

Communication between the buyer and their lender is key. The lender must be responsive, well organized, and knowledgeable about the loan requirements. He must know the applicable state guidelines for your area and have access to local appraisers. The lender is of utmost importance in moving the financial portion of the transaction along in a timely manner because once the financing process has begun, you've basically handed over control of the transaction to the lender. If the loan is not completed on time and according to the contract, the seller can sell the property to someone else and keep your client's earnest money. It's always best to use a local lender that they have a banking relationship with, unless you are dealing with a special credit union or situation where the lender is someone the buyer has used before with great success. Some of my worst experiences have been with lenders the client found on the internet, ones they had never met, but offered lower rates.

What are your buyer's needs versus wants? Now that the client has answered the initial questions and you are beginning to get to know each other, it's time to consult with them on exactly what they are looking for in their house search. Ask questions that go three deep. For example, if your client says they want a big back yard, don't stop there. Ask what about the big back yard is important to them. Will they be entertaining? Will the kids be playing soccer in the yard? Does it need to be level and cleared? Do they want a large area for a swimming pool? Do they want trees? Must it be shaded, or are they planning on putting in a garden? Do they want a fence, and if so, what kind, one for privacy or one to keep children and pets safe?

See how much you can find out about their lifestyle and how they will be using every part of the house, inside and out. This will help you eliminate wasted time by not showing them properties that won't work for them. In truth, every time you show your client a home that won't work for them, their confidence in your ability drops. So, get as much information as you can in the beginning. If four bedrooms is a must have, ask if one will be used as an office or an exercise room or will all four be needed as bedrooms.

The kitchen is the heart of the home. Find out if they prefer gas or electric for cooking. A lot of gourmet cooks prefer gas stoves because they can quickly adjust to regulate the temperature. Also, who will be doing most of the cooking? Do they want an eat-in kitchen, or do they want a separate dining area, or both? If they want an island, ask if they envision guests sitting and talking with them at the island. Will the kids be studying there while mom cooks? Knowing how the client will use the rooms in the home helps you to match the benefits of the homes you'll be showing them to their needs. Features are good, but benefits appeal to their emotions and emotions are what sell homes.

To illustrate, your client has a stressful job downtown and wants a country home where they can escape the noise of the city. A large front sitting porch is a must have feature. When you find that home with the large porch, ask them, "Can you see yourself sitting on this porch in a comfortable rocker soaking in the beautiful sights and sounds, can feel your blood pressure dropping just thinking about all the relaxing you will do here!" The large porch is a feature. The beautiful view and sounds of nature and the lowered blood pressure and feeling of calm are the benefits. Features are nice but benefits speak to emotion, and the house must appeal to their emotions before they will act upon it.

Once you have a clear idea of the kind of lifestyle the buyer is looking for in their next home, you can begin the selection process. Using the local MLS (multiple listings service), put in the criteria the items that are their "must haves." Ideally, this is done with the buyer present; search and pull up the homes on a large screen where you can look together. Select the best four or five homes that most closely fit their price range and needs.

Call and schedule the homes to view, making sure you have access and permission to enter, even if vacant. You don't want to accidentally walk in on someone in the shower! Yes, it happens more than you know! Even though you have an appointment and the agent tells you "good to go," if the home is occupied, always knock and announce yourself loudly before entering.

I want my buyers to have as much information as possible when they are looking at a home. For each home we will be viewing, I print out the MLS sheet, the tax record, the overhead satellite view of the property showing the boundaries, and a complete market analysis for that home's neighborhood. I staple all of this together and number the homes in the order of viewing with the times at the top. I make notes of which ones are vacant so if we get behind in the showings and are running late, we can skip a vacant one and go back later. Always be on time to occupied homes. The homeowner may be out driving around or running errands, waiting for the showing to be over, so please always stay on time with these.

When I arrive at the first home, I go over the paperwork I've compiled for my buyer and explain that I want them to have as much information as I can find for them so that, should this be the home they are interested in, they will have enough information to make an informed decision. Show them the tax records so they see what the seller paid for the property. Show them the boundaries and the market analysis comparing the price of the home they are viewing to other comparable homes. This is your chance to set yourself apart from other agents. I've gotten comments like, "My realtor didn't do this for me when I bought my last house. I sure wish I had this information then."

It's also a good time to bring up agency and your desire to work with them exclusively if they haven't already signed your Buyer's Representation Agreement. I will usually say, "We didn't know each other before today, so I didn't ask you to sign a Buyer Representation Agreement with me until we had the opportunity to see if we wanted to work together. At the end of today when we are through looking at properties, I'm going to ask if you want to continue to allow me to help you with your search. If the answer is yes, then we can sign the Buyer's Representation Agreement so that I am able to represent you and write the offer for you when we find your perfect home." I've never had anyone balk at signing by the end of the day. If you've been courteous, knowledgeable, helpful, and provided them with the important information they need about the homes that interest them, they will definitely want to continue to work with you.

Sometimes they may not realize how representation works. Remind them you know how excited they are about looking for homes and if they see a FSBO, a model home in a new construction community, or an open house, even though you are not with them, it's perfectly okay to go in and look around. But, it's of the utmost importance that they announce immediately that you are representing them. Instruct them to give your business card to the agent or homeowner so that if that particular home turns out to be the one they want, you will be allowed to represent them and write the offer and protect them during the negotiations.

Once you've found the home they love, it's time to write the offer. Always call the listing agent before writing the offer and make sure the home hasn't already gone under contract. You did this before you showed the property. Now call again just to make sure before you write the offer.

You will need lots of information before writing the offer. First, determine if it is an existing home or new construction. If new construction, ask the builder's agent if the builder prefers to use his own contracts or if he wants to use the standardized contracts. New construction is different from an existing home in that no one has ever lived in the home, the termite treatments are done to the soil prior to building, home inspections are encouraged but often waived, and impact fees and other special disclosures (not needed in an existing home purchases) are included as a part of the contract for a new construction home. Your broker can guide you as to what is customary in your area.

Whether new construction or an existing home, you will need the following information:

- Full name of purchaser/s
- Correct name of the seller/s
- Address of property (lot #, tax identification number, book and page where recorded or amount of acreage if larger than a lot)
- Amount of the offer
- Lender information and type of loan
- Amount financed
- Amount of down-payment
- Amount of trust or earnest money they will put down with the offer
- Do they need or want Seller assistance with closing costs and title expenses
- What entity will hold the earnest money
- Closing date (Lender can give guidelines on length needed to complete specific loans. As a general rule, 30 days for conventional loans. For VA, FHA, or USDA or other special government loans, add a minimum of 15 additional days.)
- Possession date
- Time allowed to respond to the offer
- Their name as they want it to appear on the deed

- Which appliances are to convey at no additional cost

- Do they want a home warranty?

- Will there be a home inspection?

- Is the purchase contingent upon appraisal? Yes, if being financed, optional if cash purchase

- Who would they like to be their closing company?

- A copy of any disclosures the seller has filled out for your buyer to review and sign with the offer

Once all this information has been compiled, you are ready to fill out the offer to purchase. Select the correct and most current version of the standardized form that is applicable. In Tennessee, we use the "Purchase and Sale Agreement." Most contracts will start at the top by identifying the name of the seller, the buyer, and the property address. The seller's name can be found in the tax record as the last recorded sale of the property. Note, this is 90% accurate if the tax record has been updated. The disclosures provided by the seller will usually clarify who the seller entity is. It can be a company, a corporation, or an individual. To be safe, you can use the name as entered on the seller provided disclosures.

Next, fill in the amount of the offer. Put both the numeric dollar ($) amount and then spell out the amount as if writing a check. Carefully fill out the rest of the sections being specific on the type of financing, the amount of trust money (earnest money) and who will be holding it, the length of time until closing, the response time, the buyer's due diligence of inspections, how the owner's name will appear on the deed, and any other terms the buyer needs addressed for the purchase. Spell out who will be paying for the title and closing costs, and where the closing will take place. Put a reasonable amount of time for the seller to respond.

Keep the offer as "clean" as possible. Don't put in a lot of unnecessary demands that will make the offer seem too complicated.

I recommend attaching a cover letter to the offer explaining who the buyer is and why they want the home. The seller may be emotionally attached to the property, and in a multiple offer situation, this can sway the seller to choose the buyer they think will most appreciate the home, even though their offer may not be the highest.

Always call the listing agent before presenting the offer. I generally ask if there is anything important to the seller other than price that would help your buyer to write an offer that would be a win for the seller as well. For example, an elderly couple may need post-possession to have more time to exit the home and get out all their belongings. Therefore, they may not choose an all cash offer with a quick closing because it scares them to have to be out that quickly. In contrast, another seller may need a quick closing and is willing to take less money in exchange for getting the deal done quickly. It doesn't hurt to ask. Verify that you have the agent's best email and contact information, ask them to confirm receiving your offer.

Very few offers are accepted with no changes. Most likely, you will receive a counter, and the negotiation process will continue a time or two until an agreement is reached. Remember that each time your offer is countered or rejected, the buyer loses confidence in you as an agent. Try to make your best offer in the beginning; don't plan on countering over and over.

Once you have negotiated the offer and the seller has accepted it, you are binding. What's next? There are two sides to every transaction, the buying side and the listing side. What happens next will depend on your role, and whether you are representing the buyer, the seller, or both. A normal transaction will take around 30 days to complete or close. Let's examine the elements in a basic contract.

A contract will have terms that include all the relevant information that has been agreed to. The purchase price is just one element. More often, the purchase will be financed, so the purchase will be contingent upon financing using a specific type of loan. For some loans, this means the property must be in good condition, and for all loans, it must appraise at an amount where the lender feels comfortable making the loan.

Most buyers want a home inspection and other types of inspections like termite, and continuing with the purchase will be dependent upon the results of these inspections and what the seller agrees to repair or replace. Some buyers ask for the added protection of the seller providing a home warranty. Buyers may ask for the sellers to pay for and provide a title insurance policy. Buyers may also ask for the sellers to help pay some of their closing and other costs involved with the purchase. If the seller occupies or lives in the home, the time of possession may also be negotiated. Other terms may be part of the agreement like conveyance of personal property, but those are not as common.

Let's take a detailed look at the sequence of events and steps on the buying side of the transaction that lead up to closing.

Buying side: A buyer's agent must pay close attention to all the deadlines of the contract and make sure the buyer moves forward to meet these "timelines" all the way through the transaction. You are like a conductor leading the orchestra, making sure the different players come into the performance at just the right time. Once the contract is accepted and bound, the clock begins. Every purchase and sale agreement in Tennessee that has been written on a standardized form (TAR form) contains two built-in deadlines or "timelines" as we call them in real estate. The first one is that the **buyer must formally apply for the loan** within 3 days of the binding agreement. The buyer probably has already chosen a lender and spoken with them as is evidenced by the fact that they were pre-approved. A formal application begins when the lender receives a copy of the contract to submit the application with a physical address to underwriting for approval.

You, as the buyer's agent, will need to email the lender a completed copy of the executed and accepted contract on behalf of your buyer. The buyer will provide you with the lender's contact information so you can do this. This is a good time to add both the lender and the closing agent who will be handling your buyer's side of the closing to your contact information in your transaction manager software so you can easily share documents with them. Always send the following:

- a copy of the MLS
- the tax record
- the Purchase and Sale Agreement
- any Counters and final bound Counter
- any Addendums or Amendments affecting the terms
- the Property Condition Disclosure
- the Confirmation of Agency
- the Disclaimer excluding expertise except in Real Estate
- the Compensation Agreement
- Business Affiliate Interest Disclosure
- Lead Base Paint Disclosure if applicable
- Septic information if applicable
- Personal Interest Disclosure if applicable

Always summarize the terms of the agreement and/or include a pre-filled Transaction Summary Page for the lender and closing company. The summary page has important contact information so that the lender and closing agent will know who and how to contact the parties to the transaction as needed. It's a good idea to email the listing agent and confirm which lender and closing company your buyer is using. Let them know that this step of sharing the contract with them has been completed.

The next built-in timeline is to make sure the **appraisal has been prepaid by the buyer** so that the lender can order it around day 14 after the binding agreement date. More about this later. Have the buyer shop for insurance and get a binder from the insurance company. The lender will need a copy of this and will also need to know that the buyer has finished all the inspections and "intends to proceed" with the purchase.

If **earnest money is to be submitted**, remind your buyer to write a personal check from their personal checking account to the holder. Usually the holder will be either the listing firm or escrow firm. Have them make a copy of the earnest money check for you if the buyer mails it directly to the holder. You will need a copy for your file. The timeline for submitting the trust or earnest money that was written in on the purchase agreement is the deadline for submission. May I suggest a minimum 5-day timeline for submitting earnest money? This gives you time to get it mailed and to the holder without being late. If this timeline is missed or the check bounces, the contract can be voided at the seller's discretion.

Next is the **home inspection** timeline. Most agents write in that they will have a home inspection around day 10 of binding. After that, they will have the inspection repair requests resolution within 5 days of the inspection. It is important to do the home inspection right away so that if something is discovered that would cause the buyer to want to terminate the agreement, this can be done before the appraisal is ordered, saving the buyer the additional appraisal fee of $580 or higher. No point in ordering the appraisal if the buyer no longer wants to proceed!

Provide your buyer with two or three recommendations of home inspectors for them to choose from. Advise them the home inspection is paid the day it is performed, and they will sign an agreement with the home inspector before he will do the inspection. A home inspection will vary in price from $350 and higher, depending on the square footage of the home. If the buyer adds optional inspections such as radon, it can add another $150. The inspection timeline is for completing *all* inspections, so remind your buyers to also order the termite inspection and any other inspections they want completed during the same timeline, if possible.

A normal **termite inspection** will take around 15 to 20 minutes, and prices range from $45 to $85 nationwide. The termite company will check for evidence of termites or other wood destroying insects and provide a letter stating the property is "clear." If evidence of active termites is found, the letter will make a note and recommendations for treatment. Active termite infestation must be addressed right away and treated, or the lender may not approve the loan. Most standardized contracts call for the seller to pay for termite treatment, if found, but do not automatically allow any monetary repairs for damage.

During the home inspection, show up near the end, meet your clients at the property, and introduce them to the inspector. A normal home inspection takes around 3 hours, so tell your buyers that if they come towards the end, the inspector can walk them through, explain his findings, and make recommendations. The inspection is a good time to watch and learn, and get familiar with the house they are buying.

It's also a good time to get measurements and obtain bids for improvements from vendors for such services as laying new carpeting, painting, etc. Access to the property before closing is limited to inspections and due diligence, so remind them they may not be able to gain access to do measurements, etc. until after closing! When the home inspection is completed, ask the buyers to instruct the home inspector to share the report with you as their agent so that you can assist them in negotiating repairs, if needed. Hopefully, ahead of the inspection, you have set the expectation with your clients that only safety, structural, electrical, plumbing, and health issues are asked for. Cosmetic items such as changing the paint color or laying new carpet cannot be negotiated to be paid by the seller as an inspection repair request.

A good home inspector will help guide your clients through the process and make recommendations for repairs and replacements needed. Be specific in the written repair requests. Make sure you ask for licensed plumbers, electricians, and HVAC contractors to make those kinds of repairs. Ask for help from the home inspector if you are unsure whether a homeowner or a licensed professional should make the repair. In Tennessee, we use the Repair/Replacement Proposal form (RF654) to make the repair requests, and once the agreement is reached, use the Repair/Replacement Amendment form (RF655). The latter is signed by both the buyer and seller, and it amends the Purchase and Sale Agreement and becomes a part of the contract. Follow your broker's recommendations for your state.

Once the inspections are completed and resolved, it is time to **order the appraisal.** When a loan is involved, the lender orders the appraisal and neither the buyer nor the lender gets to pick who appraises the property. Even if the seller has already had an appraisal, the lender is required to order a new one. The usual fee is just under $600 and is charged to the buyer's credit card. It is paid "outside of closing" or "POC" in real estate terms. An appraisal can take 7 to 14 days (VA can take up to 21 days), so that's why it's important to order no later than 14 days of binding. This is a built-in timeline in the Purchase and Sale Agreement in most states. Confirm with the lender that the appraisal has been ordered, have the listing agent contact you when they get the call from the appraiser to schedule so that you will know when it is being performed.

When the appraisal is completed, the lender will notify your buyer that it was good or if it was too low to make the loan. If the appraisal is acceptable, let the listing agent know the appraisal came back okay. You are not required to tell the exact amount of the appraisal, only that it was sufficient to continue with the loan process. You do not have a "clear to close" at this time, and the loan can still be turned down, even at this late stage, if something detrimental is discovered with the buyer's credit. At this point, if you haven't already done so, caution your buyers not to charge anything to change their credit. Some buyers in their excitement of getting a new home will buy new furniture to use in their new house. If financed or if there is a drastic change in their bank account, it can delay or change their credit and make them unable to close!

During the last week to 10 days, remind your buyer to set up and order their basic utilities...electric, gas, phone, water, and cable services. If any repairs were requested and agreed to, make sure to **go back and inspect** them when completed, at least 5 days before closing. Make sure the repairs are completed correctly and done to your buyer's satisfaction. Don't wait until your **final walk through** the day before or the day of closing because if not acceptable, it could delay the closing.

Walk through the house again one last time before closing. If all is okay, then in Tennessee **have your buyer sign** the Buyer's Final Inspection Amendment (form RF 660), check with your state to see which form applies to the final walk-through. Email a copy to your closing company and the listing agent. The sellers will need to sign this, also.

Advise your buyers to coordinate with their closing company and lender to make sure that all is ready for their closing. In preparation, the lender will complete the loan process and pronounce the "clear to close." The lender will email the closing instructions or closing package to the **buyer's** closing company. The closing company takes those instructions and creates the **settlement statement**. A rough draft of the closing statement is sent to the lender for approval. Then when the lender approves it, it is shared with your buyer. Have the closing company send you a copy also so you can check for accuracy.

Check to make sure the purchase price is correct, that they have been given credit for any earnest money, and look to see that the seller has been charged for any concessions agreed to in the purchase and sale contract such as closing cost assistance, title, home warranty for the buyer, etc. Check the commission, your compensation, and make sure the statement is accurate. Call the closing company immediately if you see an error or have a question. Make sure your buyer knows the **wiring instructions** for his portion due at closing, if applicable. Your closing company can give this to your buyer. Make sure they have communicated a couple of days before closing if money needs to be wired. This is best done by phone. Tell your buyers to never send bank information in an email. Remind them to bring a photo ID such as their **driver's license**. Arrange to meet them at the closing. Arrive early and bring your entire file or have access to the file in case a document is needed or a question should arise.

It's closing day! Don't forget to get an awesome gift for your clients. The more personal, the better.

Here are a few true stories from the field about working with buyers.

A Good Mule Never Leaves a Trail.

You will find that sometimes a renter who doesn't want the home to be sold may go to extreme lengths to sabotage the sale for the landlord. I was showing a home to a lovely couple, and they were beginning to envision this home as "the one." As we entered the master bedroom, the wife abruptly stopped and gasped, covering her mouth and nose and pointing to the pillow on the bed. This renter had left a soiled pair of men's boxer shorts, turned inside out, with a long brown trail right there on the pillow. It worked; my clients quickly fled the home and never looked back!

"In the World of Mules There Are No Rules."

~Ogden Nash

I had a scheduled showing with one of my regular investors to view a rental home. We arrived as scheduled and knocked on the front door. We could hear a television, and there were two cars in the driveway. Obviously, the tenants were home. Although I had a confirmed the appointment time and could access the sentry lock for the key, I didn't want to walk in and startle the occupants or risk being shot as an intruder.

We knocked for around ten minutes to no avail, and finally, gave up and headed back to the car. Out of the corner of my eye, I saw the curtains move, and then I heard the front door open. I turned around to see a 350-pound man wrapped in nothing but a bed sheet standing on the front porch grinning at me. I quickly apologized and assured him that we thought he had been notified of the appointment to view the home.

He quickly denied being notified and said it wasn't a good time, that perhaps we could come back next week. I apologized again. My investor, without missing a beat, proceeded to walk around the outside of the home, inspecting the exterior, the roof and the gutter system. He decided he did not need to see the inside because he planned to totally renovate it. He liked the location, and it was a solid brick home. Sold! I called the listing agent to write the offer and told him what had happened. He sighed and said, "That rascal knew you were coming. I bet he's been getting away with that every showing! No wonder I haven't had any offers!"

"There is nothing to be learned from the second kick of a mule."   ~Mark Twain

Another time, I was showing homes to an investor. He was extremely interested in a home in the Vanderbilt area that had just undergone an extensive renovation. The home was vacant, and the listing agent told us we could go at our leisure. We entered through the front door and began looking around the main level. As we approached the basement stairwell, we heard a loud clanging from the garage below. I yelled down, "Is anyone there?" and I started down the stairs.

My investor reached out and grabbed my shoulder, pulling me back. "Don't go down there. You don't know who or what it is and they might be up to no good." He positioned himself in front of me on the stairwell, and we heard another sound, that of the garage door opening. Obviously, someone was there. He carefully removed a handgun from his front pocket, eased down the stairs, and peered into the garage. Whoever had been there was gone. We turned on the lights and saw a stack of copper pipes, freshly cut and piled against the garage door. We had startled the thief as he was stealing the pipes from the new HVAC unit. I was thankful this investor was with me and that I had lived to learn a valuable lesson. Vacant doesn't always mean vacant. Shortly thereafter, I obtained my concealed carry permit. Agents have a dangerous job. Who else would willingly meet strangers in vacant homes? Mules have a keen sense of danger. Don't place yourself in precarious situations.

> *"My favorite animal is the mule. He has more horse sense than a horse. He knows when to stop eating - and he knows when to stop working."*　　~Harry Truman

My mother has been a real estate agent for more than thirty years. She has a lot of experience in discovering her clients' motivation. She shared this story because sometimes clients just aren't on the same page and it makes it very difficult to work with them.

An elderly couple contacted her office during her floor duty seeking a one-story condominium or townhome so they could scale back and find a comfortable retirement home, preferably all one level. As usual, Mom conducted an extensive buyer consultation and they were both in agreement on their "must haves" and "wants." The couple was pre-approved, and their current home was already under contract, they needed to find a new home quickly. Mom immediately wondered why they weren't using the agent that had sold their current home to help them find their new one. Perhaps they didn't like the service the agent had provided, or maybe there was some other plausible explanation…anyway, she decided to work with them. On the morning of their appointment, mom drove to their house and picked them up so that the three of them could ride together. They spent the day touring through several properties that almost exactly fit their criteria. However, if the wife liked a home, the husband hated it, and vice versa. They couldn't seem to agree on any of the homes and the tension between the two escalated into an uncomfortable tirade of harsh words hurled against the wife.

After three hours of looking at five lovely properties, they were no closer to finding a home than when they started. The wife asked if Mom would stop at the grocery store on the way home so she could pick up one or two items. She agreed, and Mom and the husband waited in the car while the wife shopped…for 45 minutes! Finally, the wife came out and they loaded the groceries into the car and started home. Then, the wife asked if Mom would take them through the drive-through of a fast food restaurant on the way so she could pick up their dinner. Again, Mom agreed. Finally, they pulled into the driveway and the wife asked if she could help her unload the groceries because the husband had difficulty walking. Mom carried the 10 bags of groceries up a flight of steep stairs into their kitchen. At the end of the day, Mom felt very stressed, but was more determined than ever to help them find a house, even with the extra "service" she had been called to do. She just wanted them to be happy and find a new home where they wouldn't have to navigate those stairs.

The couple agreed to look with her again in a few days. This time, the showings were going well. They toured through several lovely homes that showed promise. The wife fell in love with one of the houses and she asked Mom to write an offer on the spot! The husband said, "If you buy this house, you'll be living here by yourself." (Maybe not such a bad idea, thought Mom.) The wife fought back her tears. She seemed to want that home so dearly, and the husband wouldn't budge. He sat in the back seat, his arms crossed, determined to have his way. They started home, again stopping at the grocery store, the fast food restaurant, then hauling the groceries up the steep stairs.

Mom tried to console the wife and they scheduled another showing for the weekend.

Unfortunately, history repeated itself. The husband and wife continued to argue over every home they viewed. He refused to compromise, absolutely refusing to budge. After many hurtful comments, Mom made the decision not to work with them any longer. She felt badly for them and had hoped she could help them find a retirement home, but her gut told her they would never be pleased with any home she could find for them. Apparently, they had deeper issues than just finding a home they could both agree on. This time, instead of scheduling the next appointment, Mom apologetically told them she had a previous commitment for the next few weeks and it was better for them to not wait for her, they should hire another agent in order to meet their timeline.

The next day their new agent called Mom and asked what the story was because she knew Mom had been working with them. Mom explained that she didn't want to add to their stress or be involved in the arguments they were having during the showings…and that she had decided it was in everyone's best interest for her to stop working with them. The other realtor asked if Mom cared if she took over because she needed the business and Mom gave it her blessing. Several weeks later, after looking at almost 40 homes, the couple finally agreed on a home and bought it. And just as Mom had feared, the day after the closing they began calling the new agent several times a day, complaining about every little thing and demanding she fix it immediately. This went on for months. It was a miserable time as the couple accused their agent of pushing them into buying a house they didn't like, it was all her fault. They called her broker to file a complaint, consulted with an attorney and threatened to sue. There's a lesson here...some people you just can't help! A mule can quickly size up a situation...it's instinctive. I agree with Mom, she says follow your gut, your instinct is almost always correct! She had dodged a bullet by letting these buyers go.

"Still, I put my faith in a mule I'd met less than an hour before and remembered what the trail guide said, 'Your mule knows what she's doing.'" Barbara Presnell, *"Learning to Face Fear on a Tour of the Grand Canyon"*

(The-Dispatch.com)

CHAPTER 7

Working with Sellers
Mules Know What They Are Doing

There was a time when buying a home, living in it your entire life, and passing it on to the next generation was considered the norm. Not so much anymore. It's common rational that the average homeowner will purchase three homes during their lifetime: their starter home, their move-up home, and finally, their retirement home. In truth, research shows the average homeowner will sell their home every seven years, and this can add up to eleven moves in their lifetime. (Another reason for developing strategies to maintain your clients for life!)

Americans have learned to capitalize on their homes as a financial investment, and it is one of the largest investments most people will make during their lifetime. The average of selling a home every seven years may surprise you if you have lived in the same house all your life, but your time to move will come, too.

Why do people sell their homes? There are many reasons. Perhaps they have outgrown their home and require more space. Maybe their financial circumstances changed, and now they can "move up" and have a nicer, more expensive home. For some, they've experienced buyer's remorse. They thought the house was perfect, and then they realized the floor plan or design didn't work. They sell to make a correction. It may be a relocation, or a marital relationship change that forces the sale. There can be environmental reasons such as a decline in the neighborhood. Retirement requires scaling down to a smaller, more affordable home. Some choose to cash in on their equity. And, finally, sometimes a death or tragic event makes the home no longer enjoyable.

Whatever the reason, as a knowledgeable agent, you can help them navigate through the emotional and physical changes that occur when selling their home. Here are some basic guidelines a seasoned agent uses when working with sellers.

Before you meet with the seller at their home for that first appointment, do your homework. Study the area, look at comparable homes and get a feel for the market. Check the history. How many times has the home been offered for sale? How long did it take to sell it in the past? How many different owners has the home had? A lot of this information can be found in the old Multiple Listing Record and tax record.

Don't forget to check Zillow and see what the "zestimate" is. Even though computer automated estimates like "zestimates" are not very accurate, they are often the first information sources consumers will go to. You need to know what their expectations are. Check the mortgage amount on the tax record (the amount financed) when purchased. Are they upside down (owing more than the home is worth) on the mortgage? Is it in a flood plain, and what obstacles do you see that might present a challenge to a quick and seamless sale?

Next, get to know the seller. Begin the interview of the seller over the phone and learn as much as you can about them and their "Big Why." Why are they selling? What do they hope to accomplish, and how long have they lived there or owned the home? If they are buying another home, make sure you ask what they are looking for in their new home and offer to help with that as well. Even if they are buying out of the area, you can refer them to a great agent in that city to take the very best care of them! Come from contribution at every opportunity and you won't feel you are begging for business; instead, you are offering your assistance.

What is their dominant personality type? Review the D.I.S.C. behavioral traits from Chapter 2. Adjust your listing presentation to match their personality style. Work on establishing a connection and building rapport by adapting your style to theirs. If you are presenting to a high C personality, take lots of charts and data that show market statistics like valuations, days on the market, and trends. In contrast, if you are presenting to an S personality, be reassuring and confident and convey to them that you can sell their home quickly and smoothly, and as stress-free as possible. For a high I, let them know you look forward to working with them and getting to know them better. Share that most of your clients become friends. Assure them that you will handle all the little details and scheduling, so they don't have to worry. You've got this! Ask them to help you plan and host an open house right away. If you are presenting to a D, bring the statistics (valuations and days on market). Be assertive, brief, and to the point. Don't bother them with all the minute details. Ask them how soon you can get started and have the paperwork ready to sign during the appointment. Always ask questions in a way that will give them control. Do you want the listing to go live on the 20th or the 21st? Which day works better for your schedule?

Now that you are familiar with the property and feel comfortable with "who" you are meeting, it's time to convert the appointment and get the listing agreement signed. It's important to be knowledgeable about the listing documents and be able to explain every item included in the agreement. Arrive at the appointment a few minutes early. Introduce yourself and thank them for allowing you to meet with them. Ask to place your things at the kitchen or dining room table so you can spread out the paperwork. If they offer you a tour, accept. Be complimentary during the tour, but don't go overboard. With every compliment, their dollar sign is rising! If you are offered a drink, ask for a glass of water.

Begin your presentation with an explanation that even though they've most likely sold several homes in the past, some things have changed. Go over the steps in selling a home. Explain that it starts with signing the listing agreement, a little staging if needed, and then getting professional pictures when the home is ready to list. Next, you will upload the listing to the multiple listing service so it can broadcast to the hundreds of syndicated sites, achieving the maximum exposure for their listing. After all, the first showing occurs on the internet and 90% of people looking online decide within the first 3 seconds whether to further investigate the property by viewing it in person. It's imperative to have professional photos, a virtual tour and maybe, even drone footage and a walk-through video for higher end properties. Hiring a professional photographer and/or videographer can be quite expensive. The good news is these are direct marketing expenses and can be deducted from your taxes. Don't cut corners by using less than stellar pictures. Never use another agent's pictures from an older listing, they are copyright protected. Be prepared to spend a minimum of $500 per listing for marketing; obviously, higher end and luxury homes will require additional spending for maximum exposure. Budget for your sign, flyers, brochures and advertising in addition to photography and video expenses. Remember, there are only 4 reasons why a home will not sell: 1) Price, 2) Condition, 3) Location, and 4) Presentation. Don't ever let your presentation be the reason your client's home does not sell.

Hosting an open house is a great way to showcase your listing and gain some additional business should a buyer come in that is not represented. Discuss your plans for holding their home open and schedule it within the first few weeks of the listing. Use lots of signage and pointers and balloons and knock doors in and around the neighborhood to increase traffic and interest. Send flyers to other brokers notifying them of the event and call your sphere to invite them to the open house.

Next, discuss the scheduling of showings. Demonstrate what type of lockbox you will use and how only licensed real estate agents can access it. Someone may call from the driveway wanting to look without an appointment. Reassure your client that you'll always check with them first before allowing someone to enter. However, explain that you don't want to miss an opportunity for a showing, so it's important to keep the home ready to show at a moment's notice, just in case. Agree to handle those impromptu showing requests on a one-by-one basis, thus, giving the owner the power to decline if it's not enough notice.

Describe your follow-up procedures and how you will always provide them with any feedback from the showing. Agree on how often you will communicate to update them and let them know the amount of interest in the home. (Even if no one is calling or scheduling an appointment, you can let them know the online traffic and give them neighborhood updates of new listings and comparable homes going under contract and closing.)

In a typical seller's market if the home is priced correctly, you should get one acceptable offer after twelve showings. If the listing goes two to three weeks without a showing, then it is probable that the market has rejected the price and an adjustment is needed. Assure your client you won't let their home languish on the market, wondering why it hasn't sold. You will be in constant communication with them, updating them on changing market trends, which homes are selling and going under contract (instead of theirs), and notifying them of any new listings that would be competitive with their home.

If you haven't already, get to their "Big Why." Ask them what their preferred answer is to one of the first questions most buyers will ask, "Why are they selling?" Now, ask what their plans are after you get their home sold.

Create a list of all the features and improvements including any upgrades they have made since purchasing the home. Use the list to create a flyer to upload to the internet, mail out to other realtors, and display in the home during showings.

Discuss the average price and days on the market for their style home and note these will vary depending on the condition and amenities of the property. Usually, the market price is calculated using a price per square foot. Explain that the square footage of the home needs to be as accurate as possible for that very reason. The tax record will list a square footage measurement, however, most tax measurements use the footprint of the property and in some cases the square footage will not be accurate. Upstairs measurements may show larger as they don't take into account the sloping ceilings. A professional measurement is always best. If an appraisal has been done, they are required to professionally measure and you can use that square footage. Always identify what source was used to determine the square footage. There are also companies that advertise professional measurement services for a small fee, usually around $150 to $300. Don't forget to measure the dimensions of the interior rooms (you can skip bathrooms and hallways) as this has to be noted on the MLS before the listing can go live. Round up or down to reflect the measurement in feet. If the measurement is over 6" round up to the nearest foot, if under, round down. Now, go over the market comparables you have prepared and see if you and the homeowner can agree on the price.

Remember, the market statistics dictate what a home is worth and where it should be priced, not our opinion. It doesn't matter how much the seller owes, how much he has spent on the home, or how much he needs to get. Ultimately, the market will decide what the home is worth. If the seller is unrealistic about price, there are some great scripts included in Chapter 4 of this book to help with price objections.

A seasoned agent knows that the price, location, and style of the home will largely determine what type of buyer will make an offer. They can even predict what the offer will look like and discuss this ahead of time with the homeowner. If the home is in the price range of a first-time homebuyer

($200,000 or less), the buyer will most likely be a single person, a young couple, an investor, or a scale-down buyer such as a retiree. Ninety percent of the time the home purchase in this price range will be contingent upon financing. Even though these buyers can easily afford the monthly payments, they will most likely need and ask for some closing assistance from the seller. The average down payment the buyer would need is 3% or more, meaning he would need a minimum of $6,000 down for a $200,000 home. Closing costs will run 3% of the purchase price, also. In addition, they will need earnest money, home inspection money, and appraisal money, which is paid up front before the closing.

Most first-time homebuyers do not have $15,000 to $20,000 sitting around in a savings account. Even though their income is such that they can easily afford the monthly payments, they haven't been able to save that initial lump sum of money. They likely have school loans, car notes, and other debts that have prevented them from accumulating a large lump sum for the down payment and closing costs. A good agent will create the understanding that most first-time homebuyers will need a little help in order to buy the house. Prepare a seller's net sheet showing your prediction of what the offer will look like and include the typical concessions the buyer will ask for (title, closing costs, and a home warranty, just to name a few). Discuss with the seller ahead of time to expect the buyer to ask for these so it won't be a contentious negotiation when that kind of offer comes, and if the buyer doesn't ask for these things, then, you're a hero.

Next, discuss that most buyers will want a home inspection performed as a contingency to the purchase. Use the example "You wouldn't buy an expensive car without letting a mechanic check the engine and look under the hood." The home inspector will check the roof, HVAC, plumbing, electrical systems, appliances, and foundation to ensure all is well with the home. Even the most well maintained properties are likely to have a few items that will need corrected. For example, a ten-year old home will typically have $1,000 to $1,500 in needed repairs that the buyer may request the seller to make, unless there is a major item that needs attention (like the roof, foundation or HVAC system). In that case, it could be much higher. If termites are found, there is an additional expense for treatment. The average treatment for a 1700 sq. ft. home begins at $800.

Many buyers test for RADON. If an unsafe level of radon is found, the mitigation system installation can average $1,500 and above. Remind them you will keep the possibility of having to pay for some repairs in mind during the initial offer negotiation process, and that the final price may not be "final."

If the home purchase is to be financed, it will be contingent upon the home appraisal. If the homeowner is unrealistic in their selling price and it doesn't appraise, the loan can be declined and the buyer is free to walk away, getting their earnest money back. When this happens, the buyer can either bring more money to closing, the seller can lower the price to meet the appraisal, or perhaps, they can meet in the middle if they want the contract to remain in effect.

By discussing what the offer will look like and having the seller's understanding about the home inspection and appraisal process, you have effectively prevented the most common misunderstandings and problems that can arise during the sale of a home. Once the entire selling process has been explained and you are in agreement on the price, it's time to complete and sign the listing agreement.

In order to list the property for sale you will need the following information:

- Tax record – this will show you the size of the lot or acreage, taxes due each year, mortgages held in lien against the property, owners, flood plain information, where the property is recorded and also allow a link for an overhead satellite view showing approximate boundaries. Especially when showing land, make sure you know where the boundaries are.

- Copy of any old MLS listings – this may have helpful information you can use when creating the new MLS listing.

- Copy of the deed – the deed will reference restrictions and easements, if recorded, that you will need to know about.

- Accurate measurements – both exterior and interior

- Age of roof, type of heating and cooling, the sellers will need to fill out the applicable property condition disclosure.

- What conveys at no additional cost – do the curtains and blinds stay, what appliances will be left with the house?

- Contact information – ask the sellers for their preferred method of contact. Do they prefer a text instead of a phone call or do they want an email? Is it okay to contact them at work? You will need to be able to reach the sellers immediately when a showing is requested or if an offer has been received. (Although the seller may prefer a text, voicemail or email, never relay bad news in an email or text message. Always call or deliver an unpleasant message in person.)

- Schedule – what timeline is preferred by the seller for going live on the MLS and when is a good time over the next few weeks to host an open house? Discuss how much notice a seller requires before a showing and if the sellers will be home during the day or will they be at work.

You will need to fill out an Exclusive Right to Sell Listing Agreement or the form your broker prefers to create a designated agency agreement. The standardized form will ask for the legal description of the property, the book and page number and the address to correctly identify the property. The book and page number can usually be found on the tax record. You will need to enter the date the listing will go live in addition to the date the listing will expire. Fill in the amount of full commission, remembering you will most likely share a portion of that with the agent that brings the buyer. Fill in the items that convey with the house (i.e. appliances) and describe any special stipulations or confidentiality issues that would pertain to the sale of the home.

Other forms needed would include the applicable property condition disclosure. These can be reviewed in Chapter 5 – Know Your Contracts. You will also need a Confirmation of Agency and any other disclosures such as Lead Based Paint Disclosure, the Disclaimer notice (the agent is not claiming to have expertise in these other areas), a Personal Interest Disclosure (if the agent is related to the Seller), and a Business Interest Disclosure, if applicable. Once the forms are signed, immediately leave a copy with the Seller. Now, it's time to begin marketing and showing the property to find a buyer!

Don't just put a sign in the yard, place it on the MLS and then pray that someone will bring a buyer. That's called the three P's and this is what most agents do. If you want your listing to stand out you must think like a mule to get it noticed. Here are some ideas for marketing your new listing:

- Use professional photography and never go live until all the pictures are uploaded and you have descriptive captions under each picture. It amazes me to see new listings with no pictures. That's a sure way to be skipped over by every prospective buyer.

- Add a virtual tour. Video is the best way to attract attention. Always add a tour in with your media.

- Videography and Drones. The cost may be prohibitive for every listing but for those higher end properties use a "walk-through" video. I hired a videographer to fly his drone through the front door and out the back, then up for a birds-eye view of the valley below. It made for a stunning video experience. He also captured the breathtaking beauty of the home's surroundings and ended the video with an aerial view of the city's downtown main attractions showing how convenient the location was to shopping and businesses.

- Add your web site. Create a link to your web site to attract prospective buyers to your site. Each time a visitor clicks on your site it increases your search engine optimization (SEO) which increases your chances of being found on the internet.

- Add a video about the neighborhood or city features to attract out of town buyers who are unfamiliar with the area.

- Subscribe to major syndication portals like Zillow and Trulia and Realtor.com and allow your syndication to go public to increase your exposure. There are thousands of sites that will carry your listing, the more places it can be found, the better your chances of attracting buyers.

- Share your listing on social media. Facebook, Twitter, Linked In, Instagram and don't forget to upload the listing to Craig's List.

- Find out who is the top selling agent in the area of your listing and make sure they know about it. Email them a flyer and invite them to your open house.

- Send notice of your listing to your entire sphere.

- Door knock in the neighborhood and invite the neighbors to come tour through the open house.

- Place flyers strategically at locations where potential buyers may see it, post land for sale at the Farmer's cooperative, etc.

- Use lead capturing riders on your signage to get prospective buyer's contact information. One of the largest commissions I earned was from a "Text to number..." rider. When the person texted, I immediately called the number as it came up on my phone that he had texted for more information. He didn't buy that particular property that the rider was on, but he allowed me to show him another property which he purchased, netting me $37,000 in commission because of the rider.

- Talk it up! Tell your agent friends and invite them to tour through or arrange a caravan and lunch to gain agent exposure for your listing. Offer incentives with bonus commissions if under contract within a specific time frame.

- Advertising – as cost will allow, advertise in local paper and digital publications or magazines and other media such as billboards, benches, shopping carts, cable television, and radio. There are thousands of advertising sources that will gladly take your money in exchange for exposure.

Let's say a prospective buyer has noticed your listing and you get an acceptable offer, the buyer and seller agree and the property is under contract. Congratulations! There is still much work to be done. Here are some tips and guidelines for creating a smooth transaction.

There are timelines and performance deadlines in the agreement that protect your seller and help to keep the transaction moving forward toward a successful closing. Early on in the transaction (the first week of binding), you will want to make sure the buyer is not dragging their feet and has formally applied for the loan and the buyer's agent has confirmed which lender the buyer is using. If you received a pre-approval letter, you will have the lender's contact information. Keep your correspondence regarding questions about financing and the loan process between the buyer's agent and yourself. Don't contact the lender directly.

If earnest money is to be submitted, it must be within the timelines as laid out in the Purchase and Sale Agreement and needs to be deposited immediately upon receipt. Make a copy of the check, fill out the **earnest money deposit** form supplied by your office if applicable, and turn it into your broker. Let the buyer's agent know you have received the earnest money check and email them a copy for their files out of courtesy. They will appreciate that.

Coordinate with your seller to confirm the **date the home inspection has been requested** and make sure the seller knows it is best if he is not there during the inspection. Prepare them for what will probably be found during the inspection. (With normal wear and tear on a home of ten years in good condition that has been well maintained, they can possibly expect up to $1,500 worth of repairs requested unless a major system such as the central heat and air or the roof is involved.) Ask the seller if the home is on a termite contract (where the termite company has the home insured **in case termites** are found), and if so, notify the buyer's agent of the warranty. If termites are found, some Purchase and Sale Agreements already have addressed that the seller will pay for treating the property, but is not responsible for repairing any damage.

Once the **inspection and repair requests** have been resolved, coordinate with your seller and **assist as needed in helping the seller as he is getting the repairs performed**. You can offer recommendations of contractors and vendors that your clients have used successfully in the past to perform repairs. Remind the seller that the repairs must be completed the week before closing so the buyer can walk through and inspect the repairs. That way, any adjustments, if needed, can be made without delaying the closing.

The buyer's agent should notify you that the lender is **moving forward and has ordered the appraisal** around day 14 of the binding agreement. If you cannot get confirmation that the appraisal has at least been ordered and you are concerned the buyer or lender is dragging their feet, ask for written confirmation using email, or in Tennessee, the Notification (RF 656) form, and mark the box "seller's demand for confirmation that buyer has paid for and ordered appraisal." Don't send the notification without just cause … only if you cannot get a response. (Don't stir the pot unless necessary.)

During the week to 10 days before closing, assist the sellers as much as you can with **communication between the closing agency,** etc., and help them be ready. Get a **list of utilities** to provide to the buyer's agent. Remind them to keep their homeowner's insurance and utilities on a few days after closing in case of delays. Alarms and other services will need to be notified that the sellers are moving.

Drop **moving boxes and wrapping paper by** if you have extra to help with the packing process. I usually buy 10 new moving boxes and a stack of paper at a home supply store and drop it off for them sometime during this process. Your clients will really appreciate it. These can be recycled for the next seller if you ask them to let you know as they unpack, and you'll come pick them up (if local).

When you receive a copy of the closing **settlement statement,** review it with your seller to make sure everything is correct. Tell your seller to coordinate with the closing company how they would like the proceeds from the sale to be paid to them. Advise them not to give out account numbers or wiring instructions through email. It is better to call on the phone and speak directly with the closing company due to email fraud.

Having the funds wired to their account is best. Funds that have been wired to their account are available immediately, whereas a check may take ten business days or longer to become available. They will also need to bring their driver's license or other legal photo ID to closing.

Encourage the sellers to **leave the home in great condition**. In summer, they should mow the yard and trim one last time to make the home as appealing to the new buyers as it was when they offered it for sale. They should thoroughly clean the interior and remove all trash. Some sellers hire a cleaning service to come in and clean after everything is moved out. Remind the sellers to leave the garage door openers, paperwork, and any appliance warranties in the kitchen drawer. They will need to **write down the alarm codes for the new owners** with instructions on how to contact the alarm company to set up their own alarm code.

It's closing day! Don't forget to get a gift for your clients, or if you are giving a gift at a later time, make sure you take a thank you note to closing. The closing is an exciting and happy time for your seller, which makes it a great time to ask for referrals. Do they have any friends, co-workers, or family members that might need your help with a real estate transaction?

Once the transaction is closed and the house has sold, don't "orphan" your sellers. You have been with them for several months and have gotten to know them well. Put their contact information in your database (it should already be in there) and remind yourself to contact them on a monthly basis. They will very likely sell their home again or have a family member, friend or co-worker that needs help with real estate, and you want to make sure you stay top of mind so that when that time comes, they think of you. Here are a couple of stories from the field I think you'll remember.

When Things Go Wrong ... "God has given me a mule-like stubbornness to stick with a difficult problem and the intuitive powers to conceptualize complex hypothetical situations in my mind." Albert Einstein

I have a special client and friend who has used me for several real estate transactions over the years. There's one I'll never forget! It was November of 2015. I had their home listed, and we almost immediately went under contract. The buyers, according to their agent, were very excited because they had just sold their home in West Tennessee and would be closing within 30 days. The contract to purchase was contingent upon their current home successfully closing before they could buy my client's home.

Things happen, and I like to be careful. I cautioned my sellers not to move out of their home, lock, stock, and barrel, until we were sure the buyer's home had closed. I explained that buyers could get killed in a car wreck, go through a divorce, etc. Nothing was final until the money changed hands. So, we negotiated a full 48 hours after closing for my sellers to maintain possession of the home before they had to move out, just to be sure everything closed accordingly.

In the meantime, my sellers found that perfect next home they wanted in an area north of Nashville, closer to the husband's work and shortening his commute by 45 minutes. Our offer contained the same "contingent upon sale of home" because my sellers had to close on their current home before they could buy the next one. It was a true domino effect. The first domino in West Tennessee was the closing of their buyer's house, then my client's house, and finally, the one my clients were buying north of Nashville. Literally six families were involved in the transaction.

Fast forward to the day of closing. I called my clients around 8:00 a.m. to remind them what time to meet and again, what to bring to closing. I casually asked how things were going, my friend responding that everything was fine. They were super excited and were loading the truck right now. I gently reminded them we had 48 hours post possession, not to be in a big hurry because things could happen. The wife responded they were not worried. Everything had gone without a hitch to this point, and her mom had surprised them with an early housewarming gift ... she had paid for a professional moving company. Nothing I could say would dissuade them from loading that truck before the closing. I would be holding my breath, hoping all would go as planned.

At 1:00 p.m., I got the call from the agent representing the buyers from West Tennessee, the first domino. Everything was perfect! They were sitting at the closing table getting ready to sign. I breathed a sigh of relief, and my clients and

I "high fived," thanking our lucky stars that everything was fine. The two closings passed quickly. My clients signed all the paperwork, first for the house they were selling, then for the one they were buying. Two smooth closings. We smiled and hugged goodbye. My clients headed down the interstate toward their new destination 65 miles away. Did I mention this was Wednesday afternoon, just before Thanksgiving?

At 3:00 p.m., my phone rang. I glanced at the number and recognized the agent from West Tennessee. I answered excitedly, thanking him for a job well done. He paused and in a serious tone said, "We've got a problem." I soon learned that the buyers for the West Tennessee home became anxious during the closing process and had walked out without signing. Now, the buyers selling their home in West Tennessee could no longer perform and buy our home. I felt like someone had punched me in the gut!

"What happened?" I gasped. The agent explained that during the buyers' home inspection, the home, being on well water, had very low water pressure. The buyers had asked for the pressure to be corrected and a few other things to be repaired, to which the seller agreed. During their final walk through Wednesday morning before the closing, they turned the faucet on, and the pressure was still very low. At first, they seemed okay and the agent reassured them he would take care of it. However, the longer they sat at the closing table, the more they began to doubt if the other repairs had been done. They decided that maybe the sellers couldn't be trusted.

Their agent tried to reassure them that all could be fixed, but by this time, the buyers had changed their mind about buying the house. They left without signing and drove back home to another state.

I asked if there was anything that could be done to resolve this. Their agent said he was working on it diligently and would keep me posted. I swallowed hard and somehow found the courage to make that dreadful call to my clients, telling them that their house had not sold! I dialed their number and told them as calmly as I could what had happened. It didn't go well. How could it? There were tears of anguish, moments of confusion, raised voices. A decision had to be made immediately what to do with all their belongings on the truck because the moving company was shutting down at 6:00 p.m. Should we leave the furniture on the truck or unpack everything back into their house and start the selling process all over again?

We decided to wait and see if the buyers would somehow change their mind. The moving company agreed to leave the furniture on the truck, but there would be a storage fee of $600 to keep everything on the truck over the Thanksgiving holidays. My clients needed all their savings to go toward the purchase of their new home, if in fact, they were even able to proceed. There was no money to pay for the storage. I spoke with the West Tennessee agent, and we discussed our options. He graciously offered to pay half of the storage fee if I would pay the other half, and maybe by Friday, he would be able to calm the buyer's fears and the deal could proceed.

Looking back, I think this was one of the worst holidays I ever experienced. I couldn't relax or think of anything else all Thanksgiving Day. What a horrible thing to happen to my clients and their family! How was this going to turn out? Should I start calling everyone that had viewed their home over the first few weeks and see if we could get it sold again for them? For that day, all we could do was wait, and it was torture! Early Friday morning, the West Tennessee agent arranged to meet the buyers and the sellers at the home. The plumber who supposedly made the requested repairs and the home inspector agreed to meet with them to discuss possible solutions. The repair had required installing a captive air tank and pressure regulator on the well to increase the pressure. All this had been done exactly as agreed to, except the pressure had not been adjusted higher after the installation. It was a simple misunderstanding, and the buyers were so relieved they agreed to close immediately. Even though the closing company in West Tennessee was closed for the holidays, the attorneys opened their office and officiated the closing that Friday. By 10 a.m. Friday morning, I was notified that all signatures had been executed and the money had been successfully wired. Whew! My clients could now take possession of their new home and unload the truck!

This could have ended terribly for all concerned. There are many lessons to be learned from this experience. Things happen even under the best of circumstances. Never wait until the final walk-through to check to see if the requested repairs were made correctly. I check one week before closing! If the client lives in the home, and especially if they have nowhere to go or would not be financially able to move unless their home closes, I relate this story to them and we negotiate post-possession for the seller to remain a few days after closing, preferably at no cost, just to make sure the closing actually happens.

> *"God gave me the stubbornness of a mule and a fairly keen scent."*   Albert Einstein

A friend of mine and fellow agent, won the prize for the biggest whopper "excuse" a client ever used as an attempt to get out of a contract. My friend had a buyer, a young man, who had contracted to buy her listing and he developed "cold feet." He tried every possible way to be released from the agreement without losing his earnest money. Finally, the day of closing, in desperation, there came a phone call from his mother's phone. An obvious man's voice pretending to be a frail little old lady stated that her son had unexpectedly died during the night, so he would not be able to come to the closing! Could they please mail his earnest money check to her address? Like a good mule, this story just didn't pass the sniff test for my friend and his pretense was soon exposed.

"Picture in your mind a string of mules carrying people over a treacherous and rocky path leading down into the Grand Canyon. These people have never met or ridden their mules before today. They must trust the mule with their very life. The mule anticipates its every step and carefully places each rear foot where the front foot has just stepped."

Saitosdojo.com/whymul.htm, (a.k.a Dave's web page)

CHAPTER 8

Honing Your Mule Skills

"A Mule Anticipates
Where Each Foot Must Go"

Of all the skills an agent must master, the most important skill is to be able to anticipate what's next and the obstacles that might happen along the way. You know the steps, now it's time to carefully place your feet. Hopefully, by now you have better understanding of where your business will come from, basic real estate transactions, writing and responding to contracts, procedures and policies, and real estate law.

You've learned to recognize the most common basic behavioral tendencies, and you can mirror and match to help build rapport. You've improved both your communication and listening skills. You have been introduced to some great scripts for handling objections and are beginning the process to internalize them and make them your own. You have created a database to help you stay in touch with your sphere. You know many ways to lead generate, and you are ready to convert leads to appointments and appointments to agreements.

You know what to do, that is, what you are supposed to be doing. Now is the time to find someone to hold you accountable, someone to help you follow through with the most important activities that will grow you as a person in addition to growing your business. If you have a mentor, they can help you stay on track. If not, you may want to consider hiring a coach. Have you ever played basketball? It's not enough to know how to shoot a free throw or how to drive to the basket. You must learn the plays. You must work in the gym to become stronger, to jump higher. You must have a strategy. Imagine expecting to win a basketball game without any kind of game plan. The same is true with your business and personal growth. A coach can help you formulate your game plan and reach your goals faster and with more frequency than you will ever be able to do alone.

If you cannot afford individual coaching, perhaps group coaching would be an option. Group coaching is very affordable and you can build accountability with your peers. Partner with a peer and hold each other to the highest standard of following your group's objectives and making sure you are both moving forward every single day. Practice your scripts and give each other constructive feedback.

Develop a month-by-month growth plan for the upcoming year. Do you want to take specific classes, read more books, learn a language? Then schedule those growth activities in the month you intend to accomplish them. Plan out your vacation and block out important personal days like birthdays and holidays to spend with your family. In fact, schedule these on your calendar first and work your business around those.

Manage your time because if you don't, your time will manage you. I use a paper planner because when you write things down, that action activates a specific part of your brain that helps you remember. I also have a digital calendar that syncs with my phone and desktop so I'm never without my schedule. In this day of technology, it's easy to stay organized. You can set reminders on your phone, schedule your lead generation time each day, and then block off when you will be going on those appointments you get from your leads.

Continue learning, read lots of books, take classes, learn a new language, network, and socialize with other agents who are determined to grow. Remember, your circle either encourages you to be the best version of yourself or discourages you from trying. Surround yourself with likeminded people with a focus on success.

In case you haven't decided whether you want to be stubborn like a mule, consider this: mules are steady and stronger than their equine counterparts; they are extremely intelligent, possess a keen sense of danger and take sure-footed steps, all qualities that are immensely useful; mules don't spook easily unless they have good reason; in contrast, a horse will buck and gallop away, often losing their footing and throwing their riders off balance; mules are dependable creatures; they almost always have a sixth sense and learn very quickly; they manage their health and strength and can carry more weight than a horse; it's no wonder they are called the beasts of burden.

How to Sell, Advice from a Mule:

- Be sure footed and careful where you place your feet.
- Wear your blinders when you need to focus.
- Turn and face your fears, don't just gallop away.
- Follow the right path and keep your rows straight.
- Harness your inner strengths.
- It's ok to be stubborn sometimes.
- Plow like your life depends on it. Work hard.
- Pack your life full of great memories to carry you through the hard times.
- Learn your Gee's and Haw's.
- Know your limitations.
- Team up with other mules that will pull in the same direction.
- Don't forget to kick up your heels.

So, remember, the next time someone tells you you're stubborn as a mule, consider it a compliment. What they are really saying is you have an abundance of common sense and a strong sense of self preservation, which is why you are inclined to resist their opinion.

You now know the secret to selling like a mule. You must think like a mule and act like a mule. It's time to put your blinders on and plow through the competition and get the sales you've always wanted.

About the Author

Lisa Pardon is an accomplished and award-winning sales professional with twelve years of brokering, managing, coaching, training, and mentoring other agents in the industry. She is the owner of Muletown Realty and Middle Tennessee School of Real Estate and is an instructor with the Tennessee Real Estate Commission. Lisa is a talented presenter and speaker. In addition to being an author, she is an accomplished artist and illustrator whose work has been featured in over 77 galleries.

Lisa is a wife and mother of two and currently resides on their farm in Maury County, Tennessee, which she lovingly refers to as "The 100 Acre Woods." You can follow Lisa's continuing thoughts on her blog at https://muletownrealty. blog/

www.ingramcontent.com/pod-product-compliance
Lightning Source LLC
Chambersburg PA
CBHW060601200326
41521CB00007B/635